DISABILITY VISIBILITY

DISABILITY VISIBILITY

17 FIRST-PERSON STORIES
FOR TODAY

ADAPTED
FOR
YOUNG
ADULTS

EDITED BY

ALICE WONG

DELACORTE PRESS

Introduction and compilation copyright © 2020 by Alice Wong
Jacket design and illustration by Angela Carlino

All rights reserved. Published in the United States by Delacorte Press, an imprint of
Random House Children's Books, a division of Penguin Random House LLC, New York.

This work is based on *Disability Visibility: First-Person Stories from the Twenty-First Century,*
introduction and compilation copyright © 2020 by Alice Wong, published in paperback by
Vintage Books, an division of Penguin Random House LLC, New York, and distributed in
Canada by Penguin House Canada Limited, Toronto.

Delacorte Press is a registered trademark and the colophon is a trademark of
Penguin Random House LLC.

Visit us on the Web! GetUnderlined.com

Educators and librarians, for a variety of teaching tools, visit us at
RHTeachersLibrarians.com

Pages 137–139 constitute an extension of this copyright page.

Library of Congress Cataloging-in-Publication Data
Names: Wong, Alice, editor.
Title: Disability visibility : 17 first-person stories for today : adapted for young adults /
edited by Alice Wong
Other titles: Disability visibility. Selections
Description: First edition. | New York : Delacorte Press, 2021. | "This work is based on
Disability Visibility: First-Person Stories from the Twenty-First Century, introduction and
compilation copyright © 2020 by Alice Wong, published in paperback by Vintage Books,
a division of Penguin Random House LLC, New York"—Title page verso. | Includes
bibliographical references. | Audience: Ages 12 up
Summary: "A young adult adaptation of Alice Wong's *Disability Visibility: First Person
Stories from the Twenty-First Century*"— Provided by publisher.
Identifiers: LCCN 2021019562 (print) | LCCN 2021019563 (ebook) |
ISBN 978-0-593-38167-0 (hardcover) | ISBN 978-0-593-38168-7 (lib. bdg.) |
ISBN 978-0-593-38169-4 (ebook)
Subjects: LCSH: People with disabilities—United States—Biography—Juvenile literature. |
People with disabilities—United States—Social conditions—Juvenile literature.
Classification: LCC HV1552.3 .D572 2021 (print) | LCC HV1552.3 (ebook) |
DDC 305.9/08092273—dc23

The text of this book is set in 12-point Gamma Book.

Editor photograph © Eddie Hernandez Photography
Interior design by Cathy Bobak

Printed in the United States of America
10 9 8 7 6 5 4 3 2 1
First Edition

Random House Children's Books supports the First Amendment
and celebrates the right to read.

Penguin Random House LLC supports copyright. Copyright fuels creativity, encourages
diverse voices, promotes free speech, and creates a vibrant culture. Thank you for
buying an authorized edition of this book and for complying with copyright laws by not
reproducing, scanning, or distributing any part in any form without permission. You are
supporting writers and allowing Penguin Random House to publish books for every reader.

R0461176313

To my younger self and all the disabled kids today
who can't imagine their futures. The world is ours,
and this is for all of us.

Disability is not a brave struggle or "courage in the face of adversity." Disability is an art. It's an ingenious way to live.

—Neil Marcus

Remember, you weren't the one
Who made you ashamed,
But you are the one
Who can make you proud.

—Laura Hershey

The word *special,* as it is applied to disability, too often means "a bit shit."

—Stella Young

CONTENTS

CONTENTS

PART 3: DOING

PART 4: CONNECTING

CONTENTS

Introduction

Alice Wong

> Storytelling itself is an activity, not an object. Stories are the closest we can come to shared experience. . . . Like all stories, they are most fundamentally a chance to ride around inside another head and be reminded that being who we are and where we are, and doing what we're doing, is not the only possibility.
>
> —Harriet McBryde Johnson, *Too Late to Die Young: Nearly True Tales from a Life* (2006)

I've loved reading ever since I was young. Books were my friends, and libraries were safe spaces where I felt like I belonged. During gym in elementary school, I would sit on the sidelines and read a book. No one seemed to notice, and that was just fine by me. Writers such as Judy Blume, Laurence Yep, Madeleine L'Engle, Beatrix Potter, and Beverly Cleary and their characters made life fun and exciting even though that wasn't the case in real life.

Having had a physical disability from birth, I knew I

was different from my classmates. It took me longer to get around when I walked; I fell and lost my balance easily, which made recess scary rather than a time for play. I had some friends, but I felt alone at the same time. There were many activities at school I couldn't participate in, but I had an imagination that unlocked universes and showed me alternate realities where I could exist in new, daring, and unknown ways.

Fast forward to 2021. I am a forty-seven-year-old disabled writer, editor, and activist and a big-time troublemaker! Being middle-aged sounds ancient, but I am a total kid because so many things give me LIFE and I find deep joy doing what I want to do.

I don't think I've "made it" yet—I'm still figuring stuff out—but I can say for sure that my life got better. Two things helped me: telling my own story and finding my people.

As a young adult, I never heard many stories about or saw images of people like myself. I didn't have any adult role models who were similar to me. In 2014, I created the Disability Visibility Project (DVP), a campaign to record oral histories in partnership with StoryCorps, a national oral history organization. I wanted to expand disability history and encourage disabled people to celebrate and preserve their stories in the lead-up to the twenty-fifth anniversary of the Americans with Disabilities Act, in 2015.

What started as a one-year oral history project kept going and blew up into a movement. The DVP now has approximately 140 oral histories on record at StoryCorps, a small but mighty archive of the disability zeitgeist. And the project has expanded into an online community that creates, shares, and amplifies disability media and culture through a podcast, articles, Twitter chats, and more.

One reason I tell my own story and share the stories of other amazing disabled people is because I want the world to reflect us—we are diverse, brilliant, and unique. More important, we should tell our stories in our own words; we are the experts about our lives.

Disability Visibility: First-Person Stories from Today is my latest storytelling project in the form of an anthology, adapted for young adults from one published by Vintage Books in 2020. Later, you may want to check out that edition, which features thirty-seven stories from a wide range of perspectives. You can learn more about the book and find a free discussion guide and a plain-language summary on my website, disabilityvisibility project.com/book.

The purpose of *Disability Visibility* is to share a small snapshot of disability experience from this current time period. Each person's story is different, but they are all personal, powerful, and political. This anthology is not Disability 101 or a definitive "best of" list. These stories do not seek to explain the meaning of disability, and they are not focused on being "special" or "inspirational." Rather, they show disabled people simply *being* in our own words, by our own accounts. *Disability Visibility* is also one part of my evolving story as a human being.

Since the stories cover a broad span of topics, the book is divided into four sections: Being, Becoming, Doing, and Connecting. You will find content notes at the beginning of stories that discuss issues that may be traumatic or distressing, and you can choose to engage with the material or not. Content notes are included as a form of access and self-protection, giving you information on what to expect before reading.

Whether you are disabled or not, some of the ideas and words may be new or uncomfortable for you, and that is the point! I hope they challenge you to think about disability, accessibility, and ableism in new ways and encourage you to learn more long after reading this book.

If you are a young disabled person, I want to share a few things with you as an old kid who has been around the inaccessible block a few times:

Things will get better. Life can be frustrating and

weird right now, but you will figure things out eventually. Each person is on their own path and timeline. And if things are going great for you right now, all right, all right, all right!

You are enough. Don't let anyone ever make you feel less than or unworthy of love, access, attention, and care. You deserve everything. One of the hardest things I continue to struggle with is believing that I am worthy. Free advice: if you don't ask for what you want and believe that you are entitled to it, no one else will (unless you are a mediocre white man).

However you identify, whether you ever use the term "disabled" or not, you are not alone. And there is no such thing as whether you are disabled "enough" to be part of a community or claim an identity. This is a function of systemic and internalized oppressions. There are communities waiting to connect with and embrace you when you are ready. One of the best things that happened to me was finding a disability community on social media and in the San Francisco Bay Area. There is so much out there for you to explore and enjoy!

Disability Visibility is a springboard for you to reflect and question why things are the way they are and to take action in your everyday life. This is the book I wish I had as a teenager, and if it gives you joy and something to think about, that's all that matters. Each person has a story; it's up to you to discover yours and tell it if you want. The world is yours, and I cannot wait for you to find your power and people. To mix two of my fandoms, may the Force be with you, and live long and prosper.

PART 1

BEING

Art is supposed to make you feel something, and I began to realize my appearance was my art. My body, my face, my scars told a story—*my* story.

—Ariel Henley

I come to church happy in the body I exist in; I come to church knowing that I am not a mistake waiting to be fixed. I do not come to church with a heart that is begging for the most special part of me to change. I come to church happy and whole. I come to church free.

—June Eric-Udorie

IF YOU CAN'T FAST, GIVE

Maysoon Zayid

I was born and raised in the United States. I spent my school days in beautiful New Jersey and my summers in the war zone known as the West Bank. The first Ramadan I ever fasted was no joke. I was eight years old and on summer vacation in my parents' village. It was late June, and the Middle East is a sauna at that time of year. During Ramadan, those observing the fast abstain from food, beverages, smoking, and kissing. I have never had an issue with fasting. I'm one of those crazy Muslims who loves Ramadan.

I have cerebral palsy. That means that technically I am exempt from fasting, even though it is one of the five pillars of Islam and extremely important to the faith. The Qur'an states clearly in Surah 2, Ayat 185 that those who have medical conditions are pardoned, so I was treated like a champ for fasting. My family was over the moon, and I refused to show any weakness. I knew that by fasting against the odds I had been born with, I'd totally get into heaven and, more important, would get amazing gifts for Eid. Eid is the celebration that marks the end of fasting. Muslims celebrate for three days, because after thirty days of fasting, one day simply isn't enough.

Regardless of the heat, it's fun to fast for Ramadan when you are in a country where the majority of folks around you are also starving. Ramadan is not as much fun in America, where you are the only one fasting. In my day, teachers weren't as culturally savvy as they are now. I had teachers who genuinely feared for my life and were convinced that I was being forced by my horrible Muslim parents to fast. They'd try to slip me a butterscotch candy at lunchtime. I would shove their candy away and tell them not to push their beliefs on me. I could eat whatever I wanted at sunset, thank you very much.

Every Ramadan, without fail, my mother has given me the option to not fast. Those who cannot fast during Ramadan get to make a donation that will feed a hungry person for the duration of the holy month. If you cannot afford to do so, you should instead perform any acts of charity within your capability. My mom has donated on my behalf every single year I have fasted, just in case it ever got to be too much and I had to give up. How is that for faith?

My most challenging Ramadan came in the form of a ten-day road trip in 2011, in America's Deep South, on a comedy tour called "The Muslims Are Coming." Ramadan, which moves back ten days each year, happened to land in August. I was filming a documentary in addition to performing nightly. We would spend all day on the street doing interviews with the locals, who weren't too fond of Muslims. For the first time in my history of Ramadans, I complained. I was hot, thirsty, and tired of bigotry. Some nights I didn't break my fast until 10:30 p.m., but I survived. I broke down and broke my fast only once on tour. We were at Elvis's house in Tupelo, Mississippi. The statue of the King spoke to me and I realized if I didn't drink water I would drop down dead just like he did. I did not want to die where Elvis was born. It's okay to miss a day or five, if you are sick or traveling, or are on your ladies' holiday. You then have a whole year to make it up. Some Muslims are slick and do their makeup days in December when the sun sets at, like, 4:30 p.m. and they have to fast for only six or seven hours.

On July 10, 2013, after three decades, my days of fasting came to an end. As I mentioned, I have cerebral palsy.

One of my symptoms is that I shake all the time, just like Shakira's hips. On the first day of Ramadan 2013, my shaking got the best of me. By noon, I no longer had the coordination to tweet, and by the time I broke my fast at 8:30 p.m., I could barely breathe. I knew that I had fasted my last day. The next morning, the water I drank tasted like poison. It felt so wrong to quench my thirst during the daylight hours. Ramadan is something I strongly associate with the happiest times of my life, so I felt like a tradition was lost.

I am not ashamed that I can no longer fast, but I know many who are, even though they are excused for God's sake. I miss fasting, but I'm happy to take on my newest mission of reminding those who can't fast that there is no reason to put themselves at risk. Muslims fast so they can suffer a little. It is important not to die in the process. Instead, those who can't should channel their devotion into charity. This will not only help you stay healthy but also will help someone who is genuinely suffering. Those who are blessed with the health to fast, please don't interrogate your fellow Muslims about their hunger status. It is impolite to ask others if they are fasting unless you are in the process of offering them something to eat, and sometimes you really don't want to know the answer.

Content notes: bullying, suicidal ideation

THERE'S A MATHEMATICAL EQUATION THAT PROVES I'M UGLY

Or So I Learned in My Seventh-Grade Art Class

Ariel Henley

I am ugly. There's a mathematical equation to prove it. Or so I was told by the boy that sat behind me in my seventh-grade art class.

I'm going to stick my pencil through the back of your eye, he told me, laughing. *It's not like you could get much uglier. Even the teacher thinks so.*

Two years earlier, a different boy, whose name I can no longer remember, angrily asked me what was wrong with my face after I beat him in a game of handball during recess. *You have the weirdest set of eyes I've ever seen,* he told me. When my teacher overheard this, he sent the boy to the principal's office, where I would later go and give my side of the story, only to be told that I needed to not be so sensitive.

So when the boy in my art class continued poking me in the shoulder with the back of his pencil, I said nothing.

My art teacher that year was a heavyset black woman named Ms. J. She had a laugh so loud, it echoed down the corridor. She wore beautiful bright colors and taught us about artists and movements that I had never heard of; she encouraged us to explore what art meant to us both collectively and as individuals.

My school was filled with children who came more from upper- than middle-class families, the offspring of doctors and business executives and athletes. Though my family was well off, I felt out of place with children who were taken care of by nannies, who had fathers who attended prestigious universities and were frequently away on business trips. My father was a cabinetmaker and owned a construction company. My mother issued building permits in the next town over. Neither had more than a high school diploma. It was a town of mostly white people, so having a black woman as a teacher felt almost cultural, in a way that only sheltered white upper-middle-class children would ignorantly understand.

Every week, Ms. J required students to research an artist, a movement, or a piece of artwork that we were drawn to. *Art isn't about what you see,* she would tell the class. *It's about what you feel. Show me what you feel.* We had to research and write a one-page report explaining our topic and what it meant for our art. After school on Wednesdays, she would hold studio time, when students could come in to work on new projects and discuss the things we had learned in class. It was usually just me and a handful of other students I had become friends with.

One week, Ms. J spent the first half of class discussing the role of beauty in art and how the very idea of beauty was subjective and dependent upon the interpretation of the audience. She taught us about the golden ratio, the mathematical equation that, in many ways, explained beauty. During the Renaissance period, artists would use an equation to create balance, symmetry, and beauty in their work. It was first explained more than two thousand years ago in Euclid's *Elements* and describes a sequence found frequently in nature. Based on the Fibonacci sequence, the ratio combines symmetry and asymmetry in a way that is alluring and attractive to the eye; this is why it is often employed in design, architecture, and nature. The closer an object's measurements were to the golden ratio, the more beautiful it was.

Days later, during a discussion on facial structure and drawing portraits, Ms. J mentioned the golden ratio again. She told us that scientists had studied this equation, using the formula to quantify beauty.

"They analyze and they measure," she told us. "They measure the hairline to the root of the nose, right between the eyelids. And from right between the eyelids to the base of the nose. And from the base of the nose to the bottom of the chin. If these numbers are equal, the individual is said to be more attractive." She gestured as she spoke.

She told us that the ear should be the same length as the nose and the width of an eye should equal the space between the eyes. In order for a woman to be considered beautiful, the length of her face divided by the width should have a ratio of 1:1.618. Ms. J showed us work by Renaissance artists like Raphael and Botticelli.

I had never understood mathematical equations or ratios, so the only thing I learned from her lesson was that these were the beauty standards a woman must meet if she wanted to be deemed worthy.

Ms. J went further, telling us that additional research into the role of the golden ratio in determining female beauty reveals the translation of these calculations into an attractiveness ranking system. Individuals, mostly women, were rated on a scale of one to ten, based on the symmetry of their facial structure, with most individuals scoring between a four and a six. Never had an individual been ranked a perfect ten, but still we lived in a society that found the need to measure and rate and rank and score.

I couldn't help but think that if my appearance had been measured against the golden ratio, my formal rating wouldn't have been higher than a two.

I grew up having every flaw pointed out to me. I grew up believing I was wrong. It's part of the territory that comes with being born with a facial disfigurement as a result of Crouzon syndrome—a rare genetic disorder where the bones in the head do not grow normally. My eyes were too far apart, too crooked; my nose was too big. My jaw was too far back; my ears were too low. There were regular appointments with doctors and surgeons trying to fix me and my twin sister, who was also born with Crouzon syndrome. Some of these were for medical purposes, others for aesthetics.

I would sit in a room while doctors took pictures of my face from every angle. They would pinch and poke, circling my flaws. I would sit and let them pick apart my every flaw. And I wanted it, I did.

"Fix me," I would beg.

They would do their best.

I'd have surgery, recover, and return for more pictures, more circling and more detailing of every flaw. I was obsessed with symmetry, obsessed with bridging the gap between the person I was and the person I felt I should be.

The afternoon the boy in my seventh-grade art class told me I was ugly, I told my mother that I wanted to die. She took me to a therapist the following day.

My therapist's name was Beth. She was a middle-aged woman with curly red hair that fell just past her shoulders. She had a round stomach and round glasses and almost always wore green. I would sit in Beth's office, play mancala, and tell her of my dreams to travel and write. We almost never spoke of my appearance.

When I entered Beth's office that day, she sat facing the burnt-orange plaid couch that looked straight out of a 1975 home furnishings catalog. We did not play mancala. Instead, Beth looked directly at me and asked me if I was happy.

I did not know how to answer, so I cried. She took a tissue from the small table next to her and gave it to me, listening as I sobbed. When the tears stopped, we sat in silence for several minutes.

"It's like when you reread the same sentence over and over again without understanding what it means," I said finally. "That's how I feel about my life, about what I look like."

She nodded as I spoke, looking at the tablet and pen sitting next to the tissues on the small table. She began to reach for it but stopped. Instead she folded her hands and put them in her lap.

"I don't understand it," I continued. "These things, they just keep happening, and I know it has to mean something. It has to. I want my suffering to mean something. I want this pain to matter."

She responded by giving me an assignment. She told me that she wanted me to take a picture of my face every day for the next few weeks. She told me that I had no connection with my physical self, because my appearance had undergone drastic changes so many times. This made sense to me, and I was surprised I had never made the connection.

"You don't have to show these to anyone," she told me. "Just take them for you."

I was skeptical, but agreed.

I used to cry at the sight of a picture of myself. The tears would consume me, and I would spend the following days refusing to leave the house. Seeing images of the person I was made me angry.

I was ugly.

* * *

When I was nine years old, my twin sister and I were interviewed by reporters from the French edition of *Marie Claire*. Two women came to our home. My mother put us in dresses and curled our hair, and we sat at the dining room table, which we were allowed to do only on special occasions. The women took pictures of us and asked us questions about our lives. All I can remember of them is their accents and the way I felt confused when they kept implying that I was different.

In the center of the table sat a framed picture of my sister and me from when we were five. We were in coordinating blue-and-white sweaters and holding strands of pearls. It was one of those forced mall photos that families like to hang in their homes to convince everyone else they are happy. I hated the picture. My eyes were bloodshot, and I looked weak. It was taken only months after I had surgery to expand my skull and advance the middle of my face. They broke my bones and shifted everything forward—necessary to rectify the premature fusion of my skull. They took bone from my hips and put it in my face. I had to learn how to walk again.

A few weeks after Beth gave me the assignment, I found the *Marie Claire* article buried beneath memories and a thick layer of dust in the attic. I sat on the plywood floorboards and began translating with the basic French I had learned in school. The words spoke of the way the bones in my head were fused prematurely and described the devices that the doctors invented in the garages of their homes as a last resort. I cried as I read the words, because it all felt so simple. The way they described it, I mean. They didn't mention the weeks spent in the ICU or the fact that my mother spent her nights hunched over the edge of my hospital bed, too afraid to leave. The article didn't mention that I was a person and not a disease, and stretched across the page, in big bold letters, I saw this:

Their faces resembled the work of Picasso.

The words stamped the page right below a picture of my sister and me sitting at our kitchen table, laughing like normal children. But we weren't *normal* children, because normal children don't get written about in French magazines. Normal children don't get called ugly in French magazines.

I was embarrassed and ashamed, and I found myself wondering how I ever could have thought someone would think I was special. I felt the weight of the world on my shoulders; it felt as though the whole world was laughing at a joke I wasn't in on. I slammed the magazine to the floor and spent the rest of the night in my room.

"Picasso was an artist. You are God's artwork," my mother would tell me.

"God should take up a new occupation," I would say back.

I shredded the magazine that night.

After I found the article in my attic, I told Ms. J about it. About how my face was compared to a Picasso painting. I told her of the assignment Beth had given me and asked her if I could incorporate my project into my class assignments. Ms. J was supportive of my idea. She told me that appearance, much like design aesthetics, is arbitrary and exists only to assign meaning and purpose for those seeking it, but that ultimately our unique attributes are our signatures. They're the stamps on the world that only we can leave. They're the things that set us apart and make us beautiful.

Ms. J walked over to her desk, which sat against the wall in the front left corner of the classroom. She began punching the keys on her computer, and I stood there, unsure whether I was to follow or not.

"Leonardo da Vinci explored beauty and symmetry

through what he called the 'divine proportion.' He was a math guy," she told me, "so he frequently incorporated mathematics into his work to ensure they were visually appealing."

She turned her computer screen toward me, scrolling through an article with images of Leonardo da Vinci's *Profile of an Old Man*, *Vitruvian Man*, and *Mona Lisa*, all famously beautiful pieces. She stood behind her desk, one hand on the computer mouse, looking up at me.

"Do you know what Da Vinci looked like?" She enlarged an image of an old man with long white hair.

"I don't know about you," she quipped, "but he doesn't look too pretty to me."

I laughed.

"Being compared to a Picasso may seem like an insult, but it's an honor," she told me. "You are a masterpiece."

Today, when I think of Da Vinci, I do not think of the physical body of the man. I think of Da Vinci as his talent, as his brilliance, as his legacy. His work is often said to have been a window into the extraordinary inner workings of his mind, and it reminds me that we are all more than our bodies, more than the placement of and relationship between our facial features.

I used to find the existence of algebraic and geometric formulas that explained beauty oddly comforting, because then at least there was an ideal—something to work toward. But art isn't necessarily about beauty. Art is supposed to make you feel something, and I began to realize my appearance was my art. My body, my face, my scars told a story—*my* story. But I guess that's how life works sometimes—noticing beauty only in retrospect and poetry, in silence. Sometimes I catch my reflection in the mirror and I remember the words of my teacher, *beauty is subjective*, and suddenly the reflection I see doesn't feel like such a stranger.

WHEN YOU ARE WAITING TO BE HEALED

June Eric-Udorie

The heat of the auditorium made my head ring, and my dress felt like it was gripping tightly onto my skin. Around me were Black folk, littered in every corner of the church auditorium, their bodies pressed closely together. From afar, their bodies seemed to blend, making it hard to tell just how many people sat in each pew. It was not unusual at this time of year to have a sudden influx of new faces. The Sunday before Christmas, we celebrated Thanksgiving, where families wore matching ankara and lace and the children danced in front of the entire church, their bodies sticky with sweat as they made moves that matched the deafening sound of the drums. Beside me, my grandmother was dancing, hips swaying to the rhythms of the talking drum, her smile wide enough to expose the stark contrast between her pearl-white teeth and the dark opening between them.

I wanted to dance, too: free my limbs; take off my shoes and place them underneath the pew in front of me; join the raucous congregation, their voices gradually rising above the instruments as they sang, *Come and join me, sing hallelujah.* But I was fifteen years old, an awkward teenage girl, and my body felt like an alien shell. I was about to leave the auditorium and head to the bathroom—a last-ditch attempt to remove myself from the noisy congregation that resembled a bustling marketplace—when the pastor instructed the band to stop. He looked toward the church and announced that it was time for communion, and my grandmother grabbed my arm. There was no escape.

A deacon handed me a little plastic cup containing fruit wine. On top was a thin wafer of bread, the sign of the cross imprinted in the middle. "Dip the bread in the wine and place the communion on your eyes," my grandmother said. "If you *really* believe, if you really pray and cry out, then God will heal you."

I sighed, took a deep breath as my insides coiled from shame, and did as I was told. The words came out as a breathy whisper: *"Pretty women wonder where my secret lies."* Maya Angelou comforted me as I placed wafers soaked in wine over my eyelids, a corner of my heart still aching for a miracle. I had done this many times, and each time there was no result. I had stopped believing that God could even work miracles. But that Sunday, my bones became feeble, as if the very thing that held them together had dissipated, and I asked God for a miracle.

For a huge part of my childhood, I felt like I was a piece of clockwork waiting to be fixed. The feelings started early, with the numerous appointments to eye specialists with my mother, trying to see if there was a way to cure my dancing eyes. "It is incurable," the doctor would say, and when we got home, my mother would wail, even though that doctor, like many other doctors, simply confirmed what she was told when I was born on that rainy Thursday in 1998.

I was born with congenital idiopathic nystagmus. The American Nystagmus Network defines nystagmus as a "complex condition where the eyes move involuntarily in a small, repeated back-and-forth motion," making it hard to see clearly. Nystagmus is believed to affect between one in one thousand and one in two thousand people.

Nystagmus affects people in different ways, but it does lead to reduced vision. It can be caused by "a problem with the way the eye sends messages back to the brain or how certain parts of the brain make sense of this information." Sometimes it is linked to other inherited neurological conditions or other health problems like albinism or Down syndrome. On some occasions, like mine, it can be entirely random.

When I was in first grade, a boy at school called me a witch because I could not make my eyes swivel to the left when he asked me to. I went to the bathroom, sat on the toilet seat, and cried, tears soaking my yellow school uniform shirt, stopping only to breathe or listen to the soft whistling of the wind between the trees. That was the moment in which I learned that there was something permanently wrong with me. I was not a piece of clockwork waiting to be fixed. I had lost too many pieces and would never be fixed.

At home, conversations about my nystagmus were sparse, except when discussed as a thing that God would "deliver me" from. I received conflicting messages: God does not make mistakes; everything God creates is perfect; God corrects the things that are imperfect. With these messages, my nystagmus became a huge source of shame. I was praying a lot, asking God to heal me so that

I could have some sort of normality. When it looked like healing was not going to happen, I worked on compromises instead. I wanted to know what it was like to be able to see clearly for one day, to not trip up the stairs because I missed a step. When that didn't happen, I asked for less time: twelve hours, thirty minutes, ten seconds. None of my prayers were answered.

In 2012, an ophthalmologist at a hospital in Oxford, England, asked if I'd considered registering as partially sighted. I was stunned. The implication—the idea that *I* could have a disability—was so momentous that I didn't say anything for a while. I was learning to navigate the world as a young Black woman, and I did not feel I had the right to claim a disability. For fourteen years, my nystagmus was a thing I was waiting to be healed from, while I also knew deep down that it was a permanent state. When you are waiting to be healed, you reject a lasting condition; the idea that I could be disabled felt like I was ignoring the magic of an all-powerful god and settling for less—the conclusions of mere mortals.

Saying that I had a disability felt like I was adding ink to a penciled truth. The label "disabled" was not one that I felt I could claim as my own; it was not rightfully mine. I had grown up surrounded by people who undermined the severity of my disability, and so for me to claim the label, when I didn't feel "disabled enough," felt disingen-uous. I was Black, female, young, Nigerian, British—but I was *not* disabled. Claiming that label felt like lauding myself with an extra unnecessary burden.

It took me a few moments before I managed to pull myself together and told him I would talk to my mom. On the way back to school, I called my ma and told her what the doctor had said.

"He wants me to register as partially sighted." There was silence, and then my mother hung up. We never brought it up again.

When I stepped onto the train platform in Bath, England, all I felt was dread and fear. The fear I felt was so raw, it seemed to scratch at the surface of my skin and un-cover the truth that lay underneath. Bath was mysteri-ously quiet. It was too early on a Saturday morning, and I could almost taste the freshness of the air against my lips. The sky was a translucent blue, and the clouds seemed to stretch on for perpetuity. It was roughly a month after my seventeenth birthday and the first time I had gone anywhere on my own. I was nearing adulthood, and it felt important for me to try and confront my fears of being independent.

Now I knew the truth. I was a disabled Black girl. The truth, for many years, sat at the entrance of my throat—a lump so large that I could start breathing and living in my body only when I was finally able to swallow and accept it. That unusually warm English summer, I sat in a café in Bath, alone. I had gone there on my own. I had asked for help when I was lost, and when the person started pointing to things I could not see, I did not nod and pretend I understood. I said, "I have a visual disability," proclaiming what had been the truth since the day I was born.

That unusually warm English summer, I knew that the most important thing I had to learn—before I turned eighteen in June the next year—was to not be ashamed of who I was. The embarrassment I felt every time I missed a step, every time a friend pulled me back because I hadn't seen a car coming, was a thing I had to let go. I had to practice forgiving myself.

I took a deep breath and—alongside the oxygen and the carbon dioxide—I exhaled tidbits of the intense shame and fear that I had carried as an extra weight on my backbone. It was not huge, a trip to Bath, but it was important because throughout my teenage years, I had never been given the opportunity to learn to live with my disability and move through the world on my own terms. Everybody else around me was scared that something bad would happen. But nothing had happened, and I felt like a winner, sitting in that café and staring into the green park of nothingness.

I've been living in London for just over two weeks. The city is vast, and the people walk too quickly. You can hear the birds only if you wake up early enough, that time of the day where the sky still seems to exist in between morning and night and it's unclear exactly what time it is. This is how it is on Sunday mornings when I am walking to church, and the very city that never stops moving seems to pause a bit. When I walk into that church service, I am not the believer that I used to be. I sing over the sound of the drums, and I smile when I see other children in the congregation dancing with too much energy. I come to church happy in the body I exist in; I come to church knowing that I am not a mistake waiting to be fixed. I do not come to church with a heart that is begging for the most special part of me to change. I come to church happy and whole. I come to church free.

Content notes: language deprivation, isolation, incarceration, trauma, audism

THE ISOLATION OF BEING DEAF IN PRISON

Jeremy Woody, as told to Christie Thompson

When I was in state prison in Georgia in 2013, I heard about a class called Motivation for Change. I think it had to do with changing your mindset. I'm not actually sure, though, because I was never able to take it. On the first day, the classroom was full, and the teacher was asking everybody's name. When my turn came, I had to write my name on a piece of paper and give it to a guy to speak it for me. The teacher wrote me a message on a piece of paper: "Are you deaf?"

"Yes, I'm deaf," I said.

Then she told me to leave the room. I waited outside for a few minutes, and the teacher came out and said,

"Sorry, the class is not open to deaf individuals. Go back to the dorm."

I was infuriated. I asked several other deaf guys in the prison about it, and they said the same thing happened to them. From that point forward, I started filing grievances. They kept denying them, of course. Every other class—the basic computer class, vocational training, a re-entry program—I would get there, they would realize I was deaf, and they would kick me out. It felt like every time I asked for a service, they were like, "No, you can't have that." I was just asking for basic needs; I didn't have a way to communicate. And they basically just flipped me the bird.

While I was in prison, they had no American Sign Language (ASL) interpreters. None of the staff knew sign language, not the doctors or the nurses, the mental health department, the administration, the chaplain, the mailroom. Nobody. In the barbershop, in the chow hall, I couldn't communicate with the other inmates. Pretty much everywhere I went, there was no access to ASL. Really, it was deprivation.

I met several other deaf people while I was incarcerated. But we were all in separate dorms. I would have liked to meet with them and sign and catch up. But I was isolated. They housed us sometimes with blind folks, which for me made communication impossible. They couldn't see my signs or gestures, and I couldn't hear them. They finally celled me with another deaf inmate for about a year. It was pretty great, to be able to communicate with someone. But then he got released and they put me with another blind person.

When I met with the prison doctor, I explained that I needed a sign language interpreter during the appointment. They told me no, we'd have to write back and forth. The doctor asked me to read his lips. But when I encounter a new person, I can't really read their lips. And I don't have a high literacy level, so it's pretty difficult for me to write in English. I mean, my language is ASL. That's how I communicate on a daily basis. Because I had no way to explain what was going on, I stopped going to the doctor.

My health got worse. I came to find out later that I had cancer. When I went to the hospital to have it removed, the doctor did bring an interpreter, and they explained everything in sign language. I didn't understand, why couldn't the prison have done that in the first place? When I got back to prison, I had a lot of questions about the medicines I was supposed to take. But I couldn't ask anyone.

I did request mental health services. A counselor named Julie was very nice and tried her best to tell the warden I needed a sign language interpreter. The warden said no. They wanted to use one of the hearing inmates in the facility who used to be an interpreter because he grew up in a home with deaf parents. But Julie felt that was inappropriate, because of privacy concerns. Sometimes we would try to use Video Remote Interpreting, but the screen often froze. So I was usually stuck having to write my feelings down on paper. I didn't have time to process my emotions. I just couldn't get it across. Writing all that down takes an exorbitant amount of time: I'd be in there for thirty minutes, and I didn't have the time to write everything I wanted to. Julie wound up learning some sign language. But it just wasn't enough.

My communication problems in prison caused a lot of issues with guards, too. One time, I was sleeping and I didn't see it was time to go to chow. I went to the guard and said, "Hey, man, you never told me it was chow time." I was writing back and forth to the guard, and he said he couldn't write because it's considered personal communication, and it was against prison policy for guards to have a personal relationship with inmates. That happened several times. I would have to be careful writing notes to officers, too, because it looked to the hearing inmates like I was snitching.

Once they brought me to disciplinary court, but they had me in shackles behind my back, so I had no way to communicate. Two of the corrections officers in the room were speaking to me. All I saw were lips moving. I saw laughter. One of the guards was actually a pretty nice guy, one of the ones who were willing to write things down for us deaf folks. He tried to get them to take the cuffs off me. He wrote, *Guilty or not guilty?* But the others would not uncuff me. I wanted to write *not guilty*. I wanted to ask for an interpreter. But I couldn't. They said, "Okay, you have nothing to say? Guilty." That infuriated me. I started to scream. That was really all that I could do. They sent me to the hole, and I cried endlessly. It's hard to describe the fury and anger.

Prison is a dangerous place for everyone, but that's especially true for deaf folks.

Jeremy Woody was released from Central State Prison in Georgia in August 2017, after serving four years for a probation violation. He now lives near Atlanta. He is currently suing Georgia corrections officials over his treatment in prison, with the help of the American Civil Liberties Union's Disability Rights Program and the ACLU of Georgia. Woody spoke to the Marshall Project through an American Sign Language interpreter. The Georgia Department of Corrections did not respond to a request for comment concerning allegations in this interview.

PART 2

BECOMING

Taking up space as a disabled person is always revolutionary.

—Sandy Ho

Content notes: institutionalization, abuse

WE CAN'T GO BACK

Ricardo T. Thornton Sr.

From a statement given before the United States Senate Committee on Health, Education, Labor & Pensions on June 21, 2012

My name is Ricardo Thornton. I am here representing the ninety-two thousand people who are still living in institutions and large public and private facilities for people with intellectual disabilities—and for all of the people, like me, who used to live in an institution. With me today is my wife, Donna, and my son, Ricky.

I lived in institutions all of my childhood. I was first a resident of D.C. Village and then in 1966 I went to Forest Haven, D.C.'s institution for people with intellectual disabilities. My wife, brother, and sister also lived at Forest Haven. For many years, no one told me that I had a brother and sister. We weren't told that we were related. In the institution, I didn't get to think for myself. The staff thought for me and made all of my decisions. For a long time, no one expected anything of me. I got to know some good staff and some really bad staff. I witnessed abuse, especially of people with severe disabilities. My sister died in Forest Haven. She is buried at Forest Haven, and I still go back to visit her grave. I promised to advocate on her behalf and on behalf of others who cannot speak for themselves.

I left Forest Haven in 1980 when I was in my early twenties. That was a great day! I was in the first group to go out. I lived in a few different group homes. Living in the community was a big adjustment. Some people looked at us differently. The community didn't want us there. There was trash in the alley, and the neighbors thought we put it there until they saw that we were there cleaning it up.

At first, in the group homes, people treated us in some of the same ways as when we were in the institution. I wanted my own bank account, but staff didn't want me to manage my own money, so I got in trouble.

While I was living in a group home, I started to date

Donna—and then she proposed to me. People didn't think we should get married, but a few people encouraged and believed in us. So we got married and invited everyone we knew to the wedding. Later, we had a beautiful baby boy, our son, Ricky, two pounds eleven ounces. We are very proud of Ricky. He graduated from high school, took a few college courses, is now working part-time, is married, and is the father of three children. We were written up in the *Washington Post* and got to be on *60 Minutes.*

When I lived in the institution, no one would have believed that I could have the life I have today—married with a son and grandchildren, a good job for thirty-five years, a driver's license and car, and opportunities to speak on behalf of Special Olympics International, Project ACTION!, and other advocacy organizations, which has taken me to places like Johannesburg and Alaska and across the country.

It's important to have people believe in you and to expect that you're going to succeed. People need to have high expectations for people with disabilities because then they'll give them opportunities to learn and grow. People don't grow in places like Forest Haven.

I have been working at the Martin Luther King Jr. Memorial Library for thirty-five years, as an employee of the D.C. government. I started as a volunteer, then as a part-time worker, and then full-time. My wife, Donna, worked for more than twenty-one years at Walter Reed Medical Center and is now at the Army Medical Center in Bethesda. My brother, William, works at Catholic University. All of us pay taxes and make a difference in our jobs and in our communities. Donna and I serve on many boards and committees to make things better for people with disabilities, and we are very active in our church.

I couldn't always advocate and do what I can do now. I had people who believed in me and who supported me—friends and providers. I've seen people with severe disabilities who have grown and accomplished great things given the right support. For many people, support comes through Medicaid, which helps people live in the community and get services such as personal care, transportation, and help learning to do things like plan and manage their household. I hear people say that some people are too disabled to live in the community, but I've seen people just like the people still in institutions who do so much better in the community—because no one expects you to do anything in the institution but survive.

I love Special Olympics because they encourage us to focus on our abilities and to show off our abilities, not our disabilities. Some of the best support Donna and I have received has been from friends. When you live in the community, you make friends and they support you in your advocacy and in raising your son when you have questions and when you have to make major decisions in your life. When you live in the community, you don't have to depend on staff for all of your support, and you get to support others as well. You develop networks that you could never have in the institution. I've seen this happen for so many people, including people with severe disabilities.

When I was in Forest Haven, I had a chance to go to the cottage that had the people with the most severe disabilities, who mostly stayed in bed all day. Someone at Forest Haven got a grant so that we went in, gave people musical instruments, and played music while they played along. They loved it and never wanted to go back to their beds. When the grant ended, that program ended. If they had lived in the community, their music would not have stopped and wouldn't have depended on a grant.

When I left Forest Haven, I was asked to be on the mayor's committee on people with disabilities that was set up to close it. It was a great day when the last person left Forest Haven in 1991. What I've seen is that when people are given a chance to grow and contribute, they grow and contribute.

We ask that you ensure that people continue to be

given chances to have good lives and to grow in their communities with support. I believe that people can do anything if they're given the opportunity and support. We can't go back. We can't go back to a time when people are moved against their will to places where they have no opportunities to learn, grow, and contribute. We need to keep moving forward. People invested in me and my wife and brother. When we were in the institution, we didn't have a voice. We were thought to be incompetent, so no one took the time to teach us things. But people can accomplish great things with support. Having an intellectual disability doesn't limit what you can contribute. Being put in institutions limits what people can do and guarantees that people will be dependent for the rest of their lives.

Anyone can become disabled at any time. We are people just like everyone else. The time needs to be over for people to be sent to institutions because there aren't options in the community or because people think it's cheaper or more protected. It wastes people's lives and, in the long run, keeps them from contributing. There's no such thing as a good institution.

I'm one of many people who could be here today. People sometimes say that I'm not like some of the other people with intellectual disabilities. The only thing that's special about me is that people believed in me and in my potential to learn in spite of my disability, and they took the time to help me learn. Please protect people from places where no one expects anything from them and where they're just kept alive. We can't go back. It's time to move forward. Thank you for the opportunity to testify today and for your continued support of people with disabilities.

GUIDE DOGS DON'T LEAD BLIND PEOPLE.
WE WANDER AS ONE.

Haben Girma

My guide dog crossed the street, then jerked to a halt. "Mylo, forward." My left hand held the leather harness that wrapped around his shoulders. "Forward," I repeated. The harness shifted, and I knew he was peering back at me. Some barrier, unseen and unheard by me, blocked our passage.

Cars created little earthquakes in the street on our left. Behind us ran the road we'd just crossed. I made the decision: "Mylo, right." He turned and headed down the sidewalk. I directed him around the block to bypass whatever had stood in our way.

My dog never knows where I'm going. He has his

theories, of course. *You went to this café yesterday, so clearly you're going there again, right?* Or he'll veer toward an open door. *Seriously, Haben, we need to step in here for a sniff.*

People assume guide dogs lead blind people, and once upon a time, I thought so, too. My senior year of high school, I fretted about navigating college as a Deafblind student. Perhaps I would get a guide dog to ferry me wherever I needed to go. A companion would give me the confidence I needed.

"You want to depend on a dog for confidence?" a blind friend asked over instant messenger.

"It sounds funny when you put it that way," I typed.

"If a blind person doesn't have confidence, then the dog and person both end up lost. Don't depend on a dog for confidence. Build up your own."

So instead of training alongside a service animal at guide dog school, I spent my precollege summer honing my blindness skills at the Louisiana Center for the Blind. I learned nonvisual techniques for crossing busy streets with a white cane, baking banana cream pie, even using electric saws.

I tapped my way through college with confidence. My self-assurance didn't come from the cane but from my hard-earned orientation and mobility skills. How could I have thought that would be different with a four-legged guide?

Still, confident as I was, something felt missing from my life. My heart ached for a travel partner whose eyes and ears would share more of the world I navigated.

Maxine the Seeing Eye dog joined me for my last year at Lewis & Clark College and for all three at Harvard Law. We glided around obstacles so much more smoothly than when I traveled with a cane—imagine switching from a bicycle to a Tesla.

I learned to read her body language, and together we strode with six legs. Her big brown eyes and pointy ears opened new dimensions for me. Having a German shepherd at my side even curtailed the sexual harassment I faced. For nine years, she stood by my side.

In 2018, Maxine died of cancer. I missed her intensely, and the loss still pains me. I also knew I could not, would not, go back to life with only a cane. I was without my partner of nearly a decade, but I was not without direction.

The school that trained Maxine matched me with another dog. That summer, I joined Mylo for three weeks at the school's campus in New Jersey. We lurched over curbs and crashed into chairs, but in each new experience, through gentle corrections and an abundance of praise, our teamwork improved.

Now we wander as one. In the year we've spent to-gether, we've traveled to twelve states and four coun-tries. One morning during a trip to Park City, Utah, for a friend's wedding, I woke to Mylo bounding onto my hotel bed, ready to start the day. After a few strokes of his puppy-soft ears and some tugging of his toy whale, we left our room.

Mylo beelined for the elevator, and then, reading the braille labels, I pressed the button for the main level. The doors opened, and I directed Mylo across the lobby toward the front doors. "Right." He turned down a hall-way. "Right." He turned into a room that felt empty. "Sorry, not this one. Mylo, left." I gestured for him to go back to the hall. "Right." He turned into the next room.

The delightful aroma of food and coffee at last wafted over from the far wall. "Here it is! Forward." After I or-dered my hard-earned breakfast, another wedding guest approached us.

"Haben, hi! It's Michael. Who brought you here?"

I passed the credit to Mylo; constantly confronting ableism is tiring work. But someday the world will recog-nize that a Deafblind person charts her own path through the unknown. For now I know it—and so does Mylo. He takes his lead from me.

CANFEI TO CANJI

The Freedom of Being Loud

Sandy Ho

The day my nephew arrived, my family and I circled around in hushed excitement to take turns holding our brand-new family member. He'd arrived a little earlier than expected, but once he rejoined his parents on the maternity ward after a few hours in the NICU, we couldn't wait to hold him. All except my mother, who hesitated to reach for her first grandchild and looked at me instead of at him: "It's because of you that I am so nervous to hold him." The rest of my family, in wide-eyed adoration of the swaddled bundle, remained oblivious.

That nephew recently celebrated his first birthday, and in the flashing by of this year there was never an opportunity to excavate my mother's comment. Instead,

I have realized that wherever or however I'm confronted by stigmas of disability—and, being disabled since birth, I've experienced them often—the expectation is that my reaction should be muffled and then tucked away. But it has become increasingly impossible to do either when my life as a disabled Asian American woman is anything but tidy and quiet.

When I was a kid, my mother often retold the story of a disabled man in the neighborhood in Hanoi, Vietnam, where she was born in 1960. "He couldn't walk and would drag himself from door to door, begging. I was so afraid [that] I'd cross to the other side of the street to avoid him," she would say. A moment of sharing a childhood memory with her daughter became a cautionary tale. "When you were born, at first I was afraid of you. But then, with the support services available here, I learned to take care of you. You should be *grateful* you were born in the United States."

But what if I hadn't been born in the U.S.? What if I'd been born in any East Asian country? I wondered as a child. I never asked, maybe because I wanted to protect myself—or my parents—from having to know the answer. Now I understand the exchange of silence for the comfort of others as oppression; in this case because I still fear knowing how little value my life might hold for others.

An only child, my mother fled Vietnam with her

family as refugees to China, but by the early 1980s had emigrated to the United States—around the same time as my father, his parents, and his three younger siblings left Hong Kong for the States.

The Chinese language shaped the perceptions of disability that my immigrant parents carried with them to their new homes. It wasn't until the 1990s, for instance, that the Chinese characters used to refer to people with disabilities changed from *canfei* (useless) to *canji* (sickness or illness); the push to understand disability as a social construct has been underway for less than a decade. Media professionals in China are now encouraged by the Chinese disability advocacy organization One Plus One to use the characters *cán zhàng* (disabled and obstructed) when reporting on disability issues. But such language remains a suggestion rather than an expectation, and its impact has yet to filter out to the public.

My birth was met with the sound of a family split into opposing sides. Some relatives told my mother she should abandon me at the hospital because my disability diagnosis meant I was *canfei,* a "useless burden." Other relatives advised caution: "The heavens wouldn't give you anything more than you could handle. She is a blessing." In the end, my parents named me after my great-aunt Sandra, a benevolent woman who housed and supported relatives as they worked toward U.S. citizenship. And the characters of my Chinese name, Hoa Tien Yun, which translate to "gift from the heavens," were chosen.

I am a culmination of old East Asian attitudes and new immigrant possibilities. My identity began with an American ideology of belonging and an existence that ties me to some divine test for my parents. I cannot separate one set of meanings from the other. The erasure of disabled people is one of the most common international crimes against humanity. In 2016, a Japanese man massacred nineteen disabled people and injured twenty-six at an institution in Sagamihara, Japan. Four years later, the victims still haven't been publicly named—reportedly out of respect for their families, who wished to avoid the stigma that comes with having disabled family members.

I've answered my nagging childhood question: it's doubtful that my quality of life would have fared much better whether I was born in one East Asian country or another.

Whether in East Asia or the United States, cultural values validate the narrative of worthy versus unworthy bodies. But the entire discussion needs to be rewritten as marginalized creators and activists repeatedly point out that there are no unworthy bodies. This lodges an innate discomfort into the very core of cultural norms that are

shared by both continents: I mentally steel myself for dis-
agreements from relatives whenever I bring up headlines
of violence or oppression involving victims and/or abus-
ers who share our ethnicity. I find myself strategizing my
battles, not wanting to lose my hold on any scrap of presence I've struggled to claim, both within my family and
outside of it. Every loss or win is not a personal best kept
just for me; instead, it's a scorecard passed on through
generations and across oceans. Too much is at stake.

Taking up space as a disabled person is always revolutionary. To have a name is to be given the right to occupy
space, but people like me don't move easily through our
society, and more often than not survive along its outer-
most edges. In giving me my names, my parents—despite
their flaws and missteps—provided one of many ways for
me to access the cultures I claim. They knew that whatever paths I come upon would become mine to navigate
as a disabled Asian American—whether as Sandy Ho, or
Hoa Tien Yun, or both.

It is a privilege to never have to consider the spaces
you occupy. I come to this realization anew every time
I do the work to anchor Sandy Ho and Hoa Tien Yun to
the world, and it is exhausting to still need permission
to encompass all of myself. But in the spaces formed by
marginalized disabled people, my existence is allowed on

our shared world map in a way that is liberating simply because here I am presumed whole.

Whether I am in Asian spaces or American spaces, I traverse through life as a disabled Asian American woman. Reconciling these worlds in my mind and in my heart is my ongoing struggle to reach a place of self-love. Asking for my family to listen to me would offer only a temporary and partial resolution—it would not be enough. As a marginalized disabled person I want it all: for all of us to remain as fixtures in our shared world views, for the spaces to do more than survive, and for our voices and presence to experience the indelible freedom that comes with being louder.

NURTURING BLACK DISABLED JOY

Keah Brown

Embracing my own joy now means that I didn't always. *Hope* is my favorite word, but I didn't always have it. Unfortunately, we live in a society that assumes joy is impossible for disabled people, associating disability with only sadness and shame. So my joy—the joy of professional and personal wins, of pop culture and books, of expressing platonic love out loud—is revolutionary in a body like mine. I say this without hyperbole, though fully aware that the thought may confuse, frighten, or anger people. As a black woman with cerebral palsy, I know what it is like to encounter all three.

In 2019, I released my debut book, an essay collection called *The Pretty One: On Life, Pop Culture, Disability, and*

Other Reasons to Fall in Love with Me. While the reception was overwhelmingly positive, I did receive emails and read reviews where readers were confused, frightened, or angry—and sometimes all three. But my book is about a journey to joy.

When I created #DisabledAndCute in 2017, I did so to capture a moment, a moment of trust in myself to keep choosing joy every single day. The hashtag was for me, first, and for my black disabled joy. I wanted to celebrate how I finally felt that, in this black and disabled body, I, too, deserved joy. The hashtag went viral and then global by the end of week two. When disabled people took to it to share their stories and journeys, I was floored and honored. There were naysayers, but the good responses outweighed the bad. So I live as unapologetically as I can each day—for myself, of course, but also for those who will come up after me, who will walk through the doors I hope to break down.

Living unapologetically means that I've literally stopped apologizing for the space I take up on stages or in airports—especially in airports, since I use their wheelchairs to get from gate to gate to avoid body pain—or anywhere else I exist. I've stopped saying sorry to the people around me as the airport attendant pushes me to my gate. I feel liberated.

I may not find joy every day. Some days will just be

hard, and I will simply exist, and that's okay, too. No one should have to be happy all the time—no one can be, with the ways in which life throws curveballs at us. On those days, it's important not to mourn the lack of joy but to remember how it feels, to remember that to feel at all is one of the greatest gifts we have in life. When that doesn't work, we can remind ourselves that the absence of joy isn't permanent; it's just the way life works sometimes. The reality of disability and joy means accepting that not every day is good but every day has openings for small pockets of joy. On the days I can't get out of bed because my body pain is too great (a reality of my cerebral palsy), I write in the notes app on my phone or spend the day reading books or watching romantic comedies on the Hallmark Channel. These days and others that I carve out for self-care are necessary for my well-being.

For most of my life, hope, like joy, seemed to elude me—it felt impossible in a body like mine. I was once a very self-deprecating and angry person who scoffed at the idea of happiness and believed that I would die before I ever saw a day where I felt excited at the prospect of being alive. I realized I was wrong on a snowy day in 2016, just after Christmas, when I vowed to try to hold on to and nurture the feeling of joy, even if skeptically. I championed the act of effort and patience with myself by forcing myself to reroute negative thoughts with positive ones. Instead of saying what I hated about myself, I spoke aloud what I liked about myself.

In doing this, hope and joy became precious, sacred, a singular and collective journey. I shared my journey with the people who loved me before I ever thought I could. I shared my journey with the world because I wanted them all to know that who I am becoming is only possible because of who I was, and that is what makes it so beautiful. My joy is my freedom—it allows me to live my life as I see fit. I won't leave this earth without the world knowing that I chose to live a life that made me happy, made me think, made me whole. I won't leave this earth without the world knowing that I chose to live.

SELMA BLAIR BECAME A DISABLED ICON OVERNIGHT

Zipporah Arielle

The significance of actor Selma Blair's stepping out onto the red carpet at the 2019 *Vanity Fair* Oscars party, in a dramatic, flowing, multicolored Ralph & Russo gown and cape—color-blocked in black, lavender blue, mint green, and soft pink, held on with a glimmering choker collar—and her black customized cane, completed with a real pink diamond, can best be summarized by Blair herself: "There's a need for honesty about being disabled from someone recognizable," she told *Vanity Fair.*

In her first public appearance since publicly disclosing her multiple sclerosis (MS) diagnosis, Blair instantly became a disabled icon. As the camera's bright lights flashed around her, Blair was the image of elegance. I watched her with her head held high, her cape flowing around her, her cane in hand, and meeting the cameras with her eyes, perfectly posed. Then, as if breaking character, she stopped posing and took a step back, and her face crinkled slightly as she began to cry; her manager, Troy Nankin, came over to her and helped wipe her tears. She held on to his arm while she gathered herself, saying, "It just took so much to get out."

There I was: a disabled woman in her mid-twenties living in my parents' house in Maine, in flannel pajamas and slippers, not a speck of makeup on my face, my thinning hair held back in a headscarf, with my twelve-dollar cane I'd gotten off Amazon, watching her on my laptop. There she was: blond hair slicked back, a stunning gown with solid sweeping lines, offset by the drama of the sheer cape, a real diamond on her cane, her perfect makeup somehow flawless even after she wiped away tears, surrounded by photographers calling her name—and yet in that tiny moment, I felt I could relate to what she was feeling. It just took so much to get out.

Like most American women my age, I knew Selma Blair. Not personally, but in the way we know celebrities, from movies and magazines. I was maybe ten the first time I saw *Legally Blonde* and thirteen the first time I saw

Cruel Intentions on an iPod my friend snuck into summer camp. I know her face; I recognize her voice. To see her—a recognizable celebrity who I've known and thought of as eminently cool since girlhood—embrace her disability so wholly was incredibly meaningful for me. I watched someone with so much visibility lean on a cane proudly while displaying grace and beauty, while the photographers clamored for her attention. I felt closer to being seen—which is painfully rare in the chronic illness and disability world.

Fatigue and an ungodly exhaustion are a part of many chronic illnesses. When energy becomes a limited resource, one must become adept at budgeting it wisely—using "spoons," a metaphor writer Christine Miserandino came up with to explain living with lupus, to use energy when you have chronic illness. Blair decided to use her spoons to go out, to try and do what her body would let her do, while photographers took a few hundred photos of her—all while she was in the midst of a *flare* (or an exacerbation of a chronic illness). When she says it took so much to get out, she really meant it took so much to get out. She didn't just make an appearance; she showed up and showed out for disabled people, and for herself. The amount of precious energy it must have taken to go out cannot be understated.

"I was scared to talk, but even my neurologist said no, this will bring a lot of awareness because no one has the energy to talk when they're in a flare-up," Blair said during an interview with Robin Roberts that aired on February 26, the day after the Oscars. "But I do." She puts on a facetiously dramatic tone of voice and facial expression, and playfully shimmies her shoulders for emphasis. "'Cause I love a camera."

Her interviews since her appearance on the red carpet have done even more to bring some much-needed awareness to chronic illness and disability issues. Not only has she spoken about her specific symptoms like severe fatigue, spasmodic dysphonia, and balance issues—issues many other disabled people (including myself) have dealt with—but she also spoke out about the difficulty of getting a diagnosis. Many women with chronic illness can be sick for years before they're finally taken seriously and diagnosed. Blair told Roberts she went for years without being believed, and therefore without being treated. Blair also spoke of the lack of fashionable canes and accessible clothing, which is a problem I and other disabled folks are all too familiar with. She announced plans to release a line of accessible clothing and fashionable canes in the future. "Let's get elastic waistbands to look a little bit better," she joked on the *Nightline* interview (something that became even more relatable to me after I had gastrointestinal surgery, which made wearing nonelastic-waisted pants painful).

The embarrassment around unfashionable mobility devices and the limited selection of stylish accessible clothing has long been a problem for many disabled folks. My first wheelchair was a clunky hospital wheelchair, not meant for daily use and difficult to maneuver gracefully in. My first cane looked equally medical, impersonal, and clinical. When I've had to go out—to weddings or other occasions—and the event required I be in pictures, I often would go to the trouble of standing, holding on to a wall or the person next to me, and tossing my cane out of the shot. Too often, I went to the trouble of hurting myself, risking falling, or using enormous amounts of energy just to not have my mobility device in my shot, so as to not "ruin the photo." The first time I did it, it was because I was asked to; every other time was at least partially because I had been asked that first time. Internalized ableism is so hard to overcome partially because those beliefs are so often reinforced in society. It's not just in our heads. It's in our daily lives and experiences . . . and then it gets in our heads.

Blair decided to reject the stigma, instead opting to let her mobility device shine. She has continued to do that in other coverage: one photo in her *Vanity Fair* feature shows off a stylish horse-head cane, its designer, Asprey, named just like any other part of her outfit—as it should be.

Other things Blair is rejecting? The notion that being sick means we cannot work (you can see her in a small role in *Lost in Space* and a larger role in *Another Life,* both on Netflix). She's rejecting pity and rejecting the "tragedy" narrative that so often is forced on those who have received a diagnosis. In her interview with *Vanity Fair,* she tells them, "There's no tragedy for me. I'm happy, and if I can help anyone be more comfortable in their skin, it's more than I've ever done before." She's still working and is honest that she sometimes has to work around her illness. To then see her admit that she, too, sometimes falls or drop things is encouraging, and to do so in a manner that is so public helps both to spread awareness and to encourage those in similar situations. But this is just the beginning. Hopefully, we will continue to see more disability representation from a wide variety of disabled folks so everyone will be able to see themselves represented.

There are questions about how we consume media regarding disability. The word *inspired* is reviled by many in the disability community, who often are the subject of pity or undue praise merely for existing. But disabled people don't exist to make abled people feel better about their abledness. There is a tendency in our culture to turn disabled people into objects of what's known as inspiration porn. But for many in the disability community, particularly those who use canes or have MS or other similar chronic illnesses, Blair's public outspokenness on her reality with her illness has been both validating and inspiring. There were comments on Twitter and Instagram from people who wrote about how they'd been struggling with the decision to get a cane and how seeing Blair rock hers so confidently was what convinced them.

As for me? I have more internalized ableism to work on, and I imagine I'll have it for a while. But if seeing representation—even if it's not the most relatable representation, like from a celebrity on a red carpet—helps me (and others) accept our disabilities and mobility devices even just a little bit, then it's worth it. And for me, it does help, and it did help. I know the next time I'm at an event and take a picture with someone, I won't be moving my cane out of the shot.

PART 3

DOING

My initiation into this world revealed that disability was more than the state of my body. That idea keeps unfolding; I have been thinking about it for years, and there's still more to learn.

—Alice Sheppard

SO. NOT. BROKEN.

Alice Sheppard

"I'm broken," I say as I bounce onto the physical therapy table. My physical therapist takes some notes, and we begin. It's been years since this joke was funny. I am a choreographer and professional dancer: being somewhat broken is a way of life for me, and it has nothing to do with my disability. I keep making the joke because, conceptually, "brokenness" interests me: it is one of the defining elements of my movement practice and my thinking about disability.

Many nondisabled people attribute a degree of brokenness to disability; it arises from the medicalization of our bodyminds. To be disabled is, in this world, to experience a problem of body and/or mind so severe that it distinguishes a disabled person from a nondisabled person. I learned about my body from figuring out ways to live in my diagnosis; I learned about disability from disability studies books and from people like Corbett O'Toole and Simi Linton. My initiation into this world revealed that disability was more than the state of my body.

That idea keeps unfolding; I have been thinking about it for years, and there's still more to learn. Whereas disability in the mainstream world focuses on what my body can and cannot do, I no longer think much about ability. Professionally, I have transitioned from being a professor of medieval studies to being a dancer and choreographer. Dance has taught me to understand my body differently. My very first problem as a dancer was figuring out my chair. I had to learn how to move in it, of course, but I also had to understand what it meant as a black woman to use a chair onstage, in the studio, and in the world. This took time. In many ways, it was easier to learn how a wheelchair moves.

As I focused on actions as simple as pushing and pulling, the movements changed how I thought. I was more successful at going in a straight line with one push if I thought about my chair as an extension of my body instead of as an object separate from me. I looked to the internet to help me understand this more, but the blogs

I was reading all wanted to tamp down the stigma of a chair by calling it a "device," a "tool," or "technology." I started saying: "My chair is my legs." This was helpful in explaining to the airlines what it meant to damage a wheelchair, but it turned out not to be useful in the studio. My chair did not replace my legs; they are still there. When I discovered the concept of *embodiment*—a word I use to describe the way in which my body takes shape and form—I made another breakthrough: *My chair is my body.*

To be honest, I cannot say that this insight unleashed a fierce wave of creativity in me, but it does mark a certain place in my development as an artist, by which I mean as a dancer, choreographer, writer, and thinker. When I left Oakland's AXIS Dance Company, a physically integrated dance group, I wanted to begin an independent choreographic and performance practice. I proudly wrote on my new website:

> All my work begins with my body: as it is with my wheelchair, as it is without my wheelchair, as it is with crutches, and even with crutches and chair together. My crutches and chair are not tools that compensate for my impairment. Nor are they simply devices that I use for traveling across the studio. I understand

these starting points as embodiments, each of which has different movement possibilities. The lope of a crutch feels to me as elegant as that of a gazelle; the push of a chair creates a glide akin to skating; a roll on the floor creates groundedness and a different understanding of the spine. I want to draw out the expressive capacity of disabled bodies and minds by acknowledging and actively drawing on the movement of impairment.

It was as much a promise to myself as it was a declaration of a mission. Since then, versions of this language have wound their ways into my artist statements, choreographic manifestos, and vision statements.

I have come a long way from the brokenness of disability expected by the nondisabled world to an imagined space where the binary of "broken" and "whole" seems not to exist. I look forward to learning about the effects of this thinking and to discovering what is next.

Content notes: suicidal ideation, bullying, body shaming, infantilization

INCONTINENCE IS A PUBLIC HEALTH ISSUE— AND WE NEED TO TALK ABOUT IT

Mari Ramsawakh

If we go by commercials and consumer goods, incontinence (the inability to control your bladder and/or bowels) is a problem only for babies, toddlers, and elderly people. If we go by movies and TV shows, it might also include anxious or traumatized children. But I've lived with incontinence for all twenty-five years of my life, and I've yet to see my experiences reflected in any form of media.

I was born with lipomyelomeningocele spina bifida. While my nervous system was developing in the womb, a cyst formed on my spinal cord, disrupting nerves from my lower back downward. After a surgery to detach my spinal cord from my spinal column when I was nine or ten months old, I experienced partial paralysis from the waist down. Though I could eventually walk, stand, and bend, it became easier to lose muscle mass in my legs and increasingly difficult to build it back up. Whether the surgery improved my condition or not, I would experience incontinence for the rest of my life.

I didn't fully grasp that my body wasn't like that of other children until I started first grade. Before that, I didn't know that it was odd to have a nurse escort me to the bathroom at a scheduled time every day. I didn't know that other kids didn't have to use catheters or that wearing diapers at that age wasn't "normal." I didn't know that other kids didn't have to miss an entire day of school once a year to be poked and prodded by a roster of doctors and nurses.

But as long as I wore the right clothes, no one else had to know that I was wearing diapers or that I had a scarred bump on my back. I could pretend that I was "normal," that I wasn't different from any of my classmates. I didn't feel *disabled*, as it were. Until the third grade.

That year, when an older boy realized that what was peeking out of the top of my jeans wasn't underwear, he followed me around at recess calling me "Diaper Girl." He hounded me with questions as to why I still needed diapers and constantly reminded me that only *babies* wore them—*didn't I know that?* It was the first time I really felt like something was wrong with my body.

By the time I entered fourth grade, I was suicidal. I was desperate to be normal, but I didn't seem to fit in with my peers in any way, nor did I have the words to describe my experience. I wasn't a wheelchair user, for which I was told to be grateful. I didn't think I was "disabled enough" to let my disability hinder me. So I tried to overcome it.

I fought with my parents a lot. I told them I didn't want to wear diapers to school anymore. I said I didn't want a nurse to escort me to one of the two accessible bathrooms in the school. I thought that if I tried hard enough, I could just be a normal kid.

But things only got harder. It took me longer to use the bathroom; entire recesses were eaten up by the long process of self-catheterization. While everyone else spent their time playing and talking and running around outside, I had to go to the school office to pick up the key to the accessible bathroom, lube up a catheter before inserting it inside myself, and then return the key to the office before I could head outside. When I had to bundle up in wintertime, I could barely get all of my layers on before the bell would ring. If I skipped going to the bathroom, I would have an "accident" in class; then I'd have to get permission from the school and my parents to walk home, change clothes, and walk back.

I felt separate from and alien to my peers. I went from "Diaper Girl" to "Pee Girl." And I just didn't understand why I couldn't get it under control. I restricted my fluid intake while at school, but I still couldn't prevent the "accidents." There were even times when I had finished my entire bathroom process, but if I ran or jumped—even thirty minutes later—I was humiliated once again. Before the age of ten, I started to question whether or not I deserved to be alive.

As time went on, doctors still had no solutions or support to offer me. In high school, I started to feel too repulsive to be desirable.

If incontinence was treated as a human rights issue, as something many people face and need proper resources to manage, I could have had a vastly different childhood. Even now, shame and stigma surrounding incontinence have caused severe damage to my self-worth and interpersonal relationships. At points, I've avoided dating out of fear that I'll be left humiliated. Even in my current long-term relationship, I still wonder if and when my incontinence will be too much for my partner to look past.

I know I'm not the only person who must feel this way. Twenty-five percent of young women and 44 to 57 percent of middle-aged women also experience "some involuntary urine loss," according to Practice Bulletins of the American College of Obstetricians and Gynecologists. And doctors can't be prepared to offer long-term solutions to incontinence if they're not prepared to even talk to their patients about it. Statistics state that 50 to 70 percent of people who experience incontinence don't seek treatment for it, likely due to the same stigma I've experienced for most of my life, which can lead to greater health risks.

I've done everything I can to shorten the amount of time I use the bathroom. But the habits I've developed to do so actually jeopardize my health, increasing the risk of potentially life-threatening infections. To change these habits now would require another fifty dollars per month for the extra supplies at minimum—a price increase I cannot afford as someone who does not have access to comprehensive health insurance. If I don't self-catheterize every day, I put myself at greater risk for kidney infection and kidney failure down the road. But I pay for these necessary supplies out of pocket, and they aren't cheap.

These are important issues we need to talk about. I want talking about the danger disabled and incontinent people put ourselves in to be seen as *normal*. I want to be able to talk about my experiences without shame. I want to be able to discuss how people of different ethnicities, socioeconomic positions, and genders are affected by incontinence. But I can't do this until it's normalized to even talk about incontinence in general.

Incontinence is not just embarrassing. It's a public health issue. And until we're able to talk about it in a meaningful way, people who experience incontinence will always be isolated and putting our health at risk.

Content notes: suffering, medication

FALLING/BURNING

Being a Bipolar Creator

Shoshana Kessock

These days, I call it burning, but for most of my life, I called it flying.

It's that feeling when you're wrapped up in a writing project so hard, you look up and half a day has gone by. You haven't moved; you haven't drunk or eaten or talked to anyone. You work and work until your knuckles hurt, and there are words flowing out of you, and you can't stop until it's all done. Then you look up, realize what time it is, and fall over because the words are done for the day and you've been doing it. You've been flying.

That's what writing when you're me feels like.

Well, a lot of the time. Some days it's just normal. I get

up, I do my morning routine (take my meds, get some grub, boop the cat, check my email, mess around on Facebook), and then it's off to the word mines. And on those days, they are indeed the word mines. I check an outline; I write notes; I putter around; I get the words going however I can, tugging that little mining cart up the hill toward those far-off paragraphs and . . . Y'know, this analogy has gotten away from me. I digress.

Those are the hard days at the job because that's what it is—writing, like making any art, is a job. It's craft and talent and passion rolled up into one ball. It's doing a thing you worked hard to learn to do the best you can. You're capturing those weird little ideas rolling around in your head and making them into words, then lines, then paragraphs, and somehow they're all supposed to reach out to someone who reads them and make their brains go, *POOF, I like this.* No pressure or anything, writer, just take the ephemeral and translate it onto a page. You make it happen as best as you can.

Then there are the other days. The days when BLEH becomes BANG. The days when something just clicks and comes roaring down the pike inside my brain and it's all I can do to get to my computer because it's ready to go and that's it. Get out of the way.

I call it burning these days because that's what it feels

like: like there's an idea inside me burning its way out. But when I was younger, I called it flying. What I really meant was controlled falling. Like there was a tornado going on and I would leap off something and ride right through the middle of it, all the way up, chasing words. Because that's what it felt like for me, rolling on through the manic energy that comes with being bipolar.

A lot of folks equate the manic energy of being bipolar with the creative spark that drives artists to brilliance. They point to so many great artists in history who lived with mental illness and say, "There it is, that energy, that's what made them great!"

Except for so many artists, mental illness didn't make them great. It made them ill. And if they weren't careful, it made them gone.

When I was sixteen, I was diagnosed with bipolar II disorder.

I came from a family that didn't really get what being bipolar meant. My parents tried to get it, but when I'd do something irresponsible, it was always because I was "bad." I tried to explain how it was impossible to keep my whirlwind mind straight sometimes. How it was a battle against depression to get up in the morning and go to class. When I flunked in school, I tried to explain why; when I overcharged my credit card on a manic binge; when I cried for days and couldn't stop. But those were the bad days. And the good days—those were the days I could take on the world, when no one could stop me, when I was manic off my head. I was out of control.

I went to a therapist when my school suggested it to my parents. The therapist took one look at my behavior and referred me to a psychiatrist, a loud and overbearing man who listened to me talk a mile a minute for fifteen minutes, heard my symptoms, and pulled out a giant prescription pad. I started taking the drugs he gave me but received no explanation about what being bipolar really meant. He never explained what behaviors were unusual or what could be attributed to the illness, nor did he offer me any coping skills or resources to better understand my situation. He gave me pills and saw me every two weeks. I knew almost nothing about what was going on with me but was smart enough to realize I needed more information.

So? I went online.

I learned a lot from the internet. Those were the wild and woolly early days of the internet, when it was the nineties and everyone was in AOL chat rooms and the world was a wacky, wacky place. On the internet I found a community of role-players who eventually led me to the career I have today. It was also where I got a *lot* of bad advice about mental illness.

I read a lot of stories about people being overmedicated or given the wrong medication. I heard stories about people being committed by their families if they didn't hide what was wrong with them. But I especially came across the same story over and over from people who had been medicated. "If you go on the drugs," they said, "the creative drive goes away. You'll lose that spark inside you. If you want to be an artist, stay away from medication. It'll kill your art."

I didn't believe it. I was taught doctors were to be trusted. And besides, I knew I needed help. So I took the drugs the doctor gave me and fell into the worst confluence of events you could imagine. Because the medication the doctor gave me *did* kill my creativity. It also made me sleep too much, have no emotions whatsoever, and gain tons of weight. It destroyed my memory. And every time I brought these side effects up to my doctor, his answer was to add another pill to balance out the others, or to up my dose.

I didn't realize it until later, but I had a bad doctor. What I did know was at the height of this medicine dance, I'd spend my days sleeping or staring at a television, feeling nothing at all. I couldn't even cry. But maybe worst of all, I struggled to create. I couldn't find that spark inside me like I used to, that flying feeling that gave me inspiration. In the moments when I could feel something, it was the overwhelming terror of going back into that stupor once again.

This went on from the time I was seventeen, when I was so messed up I dropped out of high school, until I was nearly nineteen. In between, I struggled to get my GED so I could at least get into college, and then proceeded to flunk there, too, due to the medication's impossible weight on my mind. I went through so many ridiculous emotional issues I can't describe, but all of it was through a curtain of medication so thick I can barely pull up memories from that time.

The times my emotions would push through were during what I discovered later were hypomanic phases, mood swings so strong they butted through the haze and made me wildly unstable. All the while I struggled to get my life in order, and every time I did, it was under a fog of badly managed medication or through the adrenaline of mania so strong I could barely function. I didn't understand I was badly medicated, of course. All I knew was everything was falling to pieces, all the time, and I couldn't feel a solid, real emotion long enough to care.

So in 2002, in one of those moments of emotional lucidity, I made a decision to stop taking my meds. I suddenly thought, *The internet is right; this is a horrible, horrible mistake.* I trusted my experience and my terror and I stopped taking my meds.

And, well, to quote one of my heroines from the time, Buffy:

"Everything here is . . . hard, and bright, and violent. Everything I feel, everything I touch . . . this is hell. Just getting through the next moment, and the one after that."

What followed were ten years of the roughest, rockiest, most unbelievably manic, altogether difficult experiences of my life. I had bouts of going back on medication but would always stop for one reason or another. I'd make excuses, but each time it was the same thing: I convinced myself I didn't feel right on the medication. That I couldn't feel that creative spark I so relied on as part of my life. I was afraid of going back to that medically induced haze I'd been in before. I hid from it and kept riding the tornado every day. And like any tornado, my instability left chaos and destruction in its wake.

I can't say I regret those ten years. They taught me

a lot. I regret a lot of the horrible decisions I made, the people I hurt, the situations I got into where I got ripped up myself. I have memories I'll never forget, instances of realizing too late I'd gotten into something because of my mania that led ultimately to disaster.

But I remember the creative highs. The way I could just fly like the wind and produce twelve thousand words in a night. How I could map out entire novels, series of books, all the things in the world I thought I could create. I wrote papers, read whole book series, stayed up for days on end, played role-playing games from morning until night, and never, ever saw anything wrong with where I was in life. Because I was living that artist's life and I thought, *Hey, this is me. This is who I am.*

I now know the truth: that was the illness talking. The "living high on life, throwing caution to the winds" voice *is* the manic voice. And unless tempered with medication and coping mechanisms, it can lead to disaster.

From 2002 until 2012 I remained largely unmedicated. And those ten years are, in hindsight, an unspoken cautionary tale of someone not flying but falling without recognizing the drop in altitude. A tale of someone on a corkscrew through rough weather, catching fire all the way down.

I went to grad school in 2012, and thank god for so

many reasons that I did. It's not even my education I laud when I think of those years, but a single day in November 2012. I'd only been in classes for two months and already I was starting to lose it from the stress. The day I broke down with a massive anxiety attack after a critique from a teacher, hiccupping with tears and hyperventilating in a bathroom, I walked across the street to the health clinic and got an appointment with a mental health counselor. There a very nice man named Bob talked to me about my experiences, about what I knew about bipolar disorder.

Bob told me some truth about where I was at and what I needed. He said he was surprised I'd gotten as far as I did going the way I had been. He listened to my fears about going on meds and what happened in the past. Then he calmly explained how he was going to give me medication and we'd work together to find what worked.

The first day after I took medication, I woke up in the morning and the tornado was quieter. Not quiet, but less a twisting funnel of noise and more of a loud echo. I called up someone who was then a friend (who had experience with the medication I'd started taking) and broke down crying. I asked him: Is this what normal feels like? I had no idea it would get even better.

Six years later, I've never been off my medication a single day. And I've graduated from grad school, survived a brain surgery and being diagnosed with two serious chronic illnesses, ended up using a wheelchair, run my own business, and become a writer, with too many personal ups and downs to count. Each of them I tackled with a surety in myself I could never have had before, because I was no longer screaming through a tornado all the time. More important, I've spent those years creating games and writing work I've made with deliberateness and careful consideration. When I create, it is no longer controlled falling, but dedicated flight on a controlled course. Well, most of the time.

I won't say everything became perfect after I started medication. Being bipolar is a constant system of checks and balances. These days I fight against needing my medication adjusted a lot, against depression and anxiety, mania and hypomania. I still end up flying some days, sometimes for days at a time, because as time goes on, the body changes and you have to adjust to new needs, new doses, new medication.

Coping mechanisms change, life situations go ways you never expected, mania and depression rear their ugly heads. But the day I went on medication was one of the greatest days of my life, because it was the day my creative spark stopped becoming an excuse to keep putting up with an illness that was killing me.

I did some research online (now responsibly!) about artists who were known to have fought mental illness. Google it sometime; it'll be a stark look into some suffering for art you might not know about. People know about Vincent van Gogh, the artist who suffered during his life from mental illness, self-medicated, was treated by doctors, and struggled to succeed despite his obvious impossible talent due to his sickness, but what about Beethoven and David Foster Wallace, Georgia O'Keeffe and Sylvia Plath, Francisco Goya and Kurt Cobain, Robin Williams and Amy Winehouse? I did research and discovered artists like Mariah Carey, Demi Lovato, Catherine Zeta-Jones, Vivien Leigh, Russell Brand, Linda Hamilton, and of course Carrie Fisher all have/had bipolar disorder. Their stories, their struggles, are well known.

I read books about people theorizing about the connection between mental illness and creativity and shake my head. I don't need to know the connection, because if there is one, it doesn't matter to me. I take my medicine and work my craft at the same time because I don't need to suffer as an artist. I don't need the mania to take flight and reach inspiration. I can do that on my own.

Mental illness and the struggle against it is one I'll

tackle for the rest of my life. The day I started my journey to getting better by taking medication—by denying the world my suffering and instead giving myself permission to live healthier while making art—was the day I started rebuilding myself into the strongest version of me. Every day, one more brick, with every word I write, I build myself higher.

GAINING POWER THROUGH COMMUNICATION ACCESS

Lateef McLeod

*F*rom *"Assistive Technology," episode three of the podcast* Disability Visibility, *first aired in October 2017*

LATEEF MCLEOD: [typing] My . . . name is . . . Lateef . . . McLeod. My name is Lateef McLeod. I am currently a doctoral student in the Anthropology and Social Change program at California Institute of Integral Studies. I plan to concentrate my studies on how people with significant disabilities can acquire more political and social power within this society. More media exposure is part of this acquiring of power. That is why your podcast is important, along with my writing. I am in the process of writing another poetry book and a novel where I will be highlighting more disability issues. I am also busy doing advocacy work at my church, Allen Temple Baptist Church, in the Persons with Disabilities Ministry and with the International Society for Augmentative and Alternative Communication, where I am lead committee chair.

ALICE WONG: So, Lateef, tell me a little bit about the types of assistive technology that you use and that you can't live without.

LATEEF: [typing] The assistive technologies that I cannot live without are my power wheelchair, because that is how I get around, and the Proloquo2Go and Proloquo4Text apps on my iPad and my iPhone, because that is how I communicate.

ALICE: Yep, I'm in a power chair, too. And without my computer and without my wheelchair, I would be stuck at home. They're pretty much essential to my life.

LATEEF: [typing] Yes. Yes, and of course I cannot live without my laptop.

ALICE: So we're talking about assistive technology, especially ones that assist with communication. What is augmentative and alternative communication, for people who've never heard of that term? It's also known as AAC.

LATEEF: Augmentative and alternative communication is nonverbal communication for people with speech disabilities, using symbols, letters, and words on low-tech and high-tech devices.

ALICE: And how have you used AAC throughout your life? Was it all throughout your life or only later, as you got a little older?

LATEEF: [typing] I started using AAC when I was six and obtained my first Touch Talker.

ALICE: Obviously, you've seen a lot of changes throughout the years with AAC and other forms of assistive technology. As you grew up, what was it like using all the different kinds of devices as time has gone on? What have you observed and experienced?

LATEEF: [typing] The main difference between my iPad and my other AAC devices is that the iPad is mass-produced and, as a result, is much more inexpensive than the AAC devices that I had before that were produced specifically for people with complex communication needs. As a result, my other devices were thousands of dollars compared to my iPad, which was hundreds of dollars.

ALICE: Yeah, definitely I think the lean toward universal design has really put the AAC and other forms of assistive technology in the hands of disabled people, many of whom do not have money or [who] might not have insurance to cover devices and technology like this. What do you think can be done to get more iPads and other forms of assistive technology to nonspeaking disabled people who really need it?

LATEEF: I think devices need to be more integrated with other devices people normally buy, like phones, tablets, and computers, so that the overhead cost will come down.

ALICE: I totally agree with you. There's this rehabilitation-industrial complex where some of these devices you used in the past were designed and created for people with complex disabilities that's medicalized, and technology is so much more than that. And for me, the stuff that I used in the past that was designed for us is usually not only, like you said, very expensive, but it's often very ugly and not the easiest to use. And very rarely are these kinds of technology and devices created by disabled people, but that's slowly changing.

[upbeat electronica]

Can you tell me about an example of, let's say, before iPads, before iPhones, before Wi-Fi and laptops, a device that you used for AAC that did what you needed to do but that you really kinda didn't like or that was really difficult to use?

LATEEF: One of my first devices was called Touch Talker, and it was a bulky thing with picture icons on it. And I had to remember picture sequences to access instant phrases. But I always would forget the phrases and would just spell everything out.

ALICE: Yeah, I imagine that you had to remember a lot of things, depending on the device, because they're so limited and you have limited choices.

So, you mentioned you were six when you first started using AAC. Do you remember what life was like before you started using AAC and other forms of technology like this?

LATEEF: Before I acquired my first AAC device, which was a Touch Talker, my mom made picture boards where I could point to different words. I also could vocalize simple words and could perform rudimentary sign language.

ALICE: What do you think is the importance of AAC and other forms of assistive technology for people with disabilities, as you've seen in your own life and with people in the disability community?

LATEEF: [typing] The importance of AAC should be obvious, because it allows people who have complex communication needs to express themselves and interact with people in their community.

ALICE: Absolutely. If you had a wish list, what improvements would you like with the tech you're using right now?

LATEEF: The most important issue that I think needs to be addressed is more availability of AAC devices to those who need them at a more affordable price. I would like to make sure that everyone who needs a device has one.

ALICE: Yeah, I think the line between technology and assistive technology is really blurry, right? Everybody who has an iPhone can use Siri, and Siri is a form of assistive technology for a lot of people with disabilities. . . . When more people think of it as a standard feature, it could only help everyone. Is there anything you would like to see in the future that you would really benefit from but that you haven't seen yet?

LATEEF: I would like to have a vocal ID for my AAC devices, because they are advertised to produce a more personalized digital voice that will sound like the particular user.

ALICE: Mm, yeah, that would be nice. It would be really nice to have a customized voice to really reflect your personality, 'cause that must be pretty challenging, to get the full expression of your emotions and personality from a device that sounds somewhat standardized.

LATEEF: People who have AAC definitely have a lot of issues beyond acquiring the right AAC so that we can communicate. Some of us have severe mobility disabilities as well. So that further marginalizes us in our community. Because of our challenges with communication, we face more seclusion and isolation than other members of the population.

So what I am studying now in my graduate program is how people who use AAC can gain the social and political power to be more included and engaged in society. We need more than technology to fix this problem; we need to change the consciousness of society to be more accepting to people who use AAC.

ALICE: I totally agree with you! Lateef, you're also a poet, and I was wondering if you can share one that I really love, "I Am Too Pretty for Some 'Ugly Laws'"?

LATEEF:
I am not supposed to be here
in this body,
here
speaking to you.
My mere presence
of erratic moving limbs
and drooling smile
used to be scrubbed
off the public pavement.
Ugly laws used to be
on many U.S. cities' lawbooks,

beginning in Chicago in 1867,
stating that "any person who is
diseased, maimed, mutilated,
or in any way deformed
so as to be an unsightly or disgusting object,
or an improper person to be allowed
in or on the streets, highways, thoroughfares,
or public places in this city,
shall not therein or thereon
expose himself to public view,
under the penalty of $1 for each offense."
Any person who looked like me
was deemed disgusting
and was locked away
from the eyes of the upstanding citizens.
I am too pretty for some Ugly Laws,
Too smooth to be shut in.
Too smart and eclectic
for any box you put me in.
My swagger is too bold
to be swept up in these public streets.
You can stare at me all you want.
No cop will bust in my head
and carry me away to an institution.
No doctor will diagnose me

a helpless invalid with an incurable disease.
No angry mob with clubs and torches
will try to run me out of town.
Whatever you do,
my roots are rigid
like a hundred-year-old tree.
I will stay right here
to glare at your ugly face, too.

PART 4

CONNECTING

My ancestors are disabled people who lived looking
out of institution windows, wanting so much more
for themselves. . . . All of my ancestors know
longing. Longing is often our connecting place.

—Stacey Milbern

THE FEARLESS BENJAMIN LAY

Activist, Abolitionist, Dwarf Person

Eugene Grant

I didn't learn of Benjamin Lay until I was thirty-one years old. This is important, because I myself have dwarfism. There is a shameful absence of books documenting the lives of important historical figures with dwarfism. Just as *Game of Thrones* and Tyrion Lannister alone cannot compensate—as many people of average height seem to think he does—for centuries of ridicule and abuse, so Marcus Rediker and *The Fearless Benjamin Lay* cannot make up for this dearth of representation, but the book is a significant step forward.

Who was Benjamin Lay? Born in England in 1682, Lay was one of the first white radical abolitionists. An autodidact, he was a sailor, glove maker, bookseller, and author. He wrote one of the world's first abolitionist texts, *All Slave-Keepers That Keep the Innocent in Bondage, Apostates*. A devout Quaker, Lay loudly called for the church to cast out slave owners. He boycotted slave-produced commodities.

His time at sea, and particularly his experiences in Barbados, fueled his hatred of slavery, and he later became notorious for theatrical protests at Quaker meetings. In one spectacular demonstration, in 1738 at the Philadelphia Yearly Meeting, he hid a bladder filled with red juice inside a book, then ran his sword through the text, spattering "blood" on the stunned slave owners present.

At the time, many Quakers resisted Lay's abolitionist views. Just as Lay had called for slave keepers to be cast out of the church, they cast him out of his. They disowned him. They denounced his book. They stopped him speaking at meetings—often physically removing him from the premises. They even withheld his marriage certificate to his wife, Sarah.

While talking and tweeting about Lay's life, I encountered those who—in good will, I'm sure—thought it best to celebrate Lay's achievements without mentioning his dwarfism. Such views take shape in a world where so many are taught that dwarfism is at best undesirable and at worst to be feared or loathed. To erase Lay's dwarfism would be, some might think, to "make him normal."

But life in a dwarf body shaped Lay's beliefs. At times, he struggled to be considered equal—a battle many dwarf people still face today. In one incident, Rediker records how a man of average height tried to humiliate Lay by approaching him and announcing: "I am your servant." With razor-sharp repartee, Lay stuck out his foot and replied, "Then clean my shoe," embarrassing the bully. To erase his dwarfism would limit our view of his life. It would sever a connection between Lay and his wife, herself a dwarf person. And it was life in a dwarf body that led some historians, Rediker notes, to dismiss Lay as "a little hunchback," sustaining his obscurity.

There is another vital reason why we must keep Lay's dwarfism at the heart of discussions about him: because pernicious stereotypes dominate representations of dwarf people. A film about Lay's life is yet to be made, but movies like *Austin Powers* and *Wolf of Wall Street*—which sustain the spectacle of dwarf bodies and condone violence toward them (violence then reenacted in real life)—gross hundreds of millions of dollars. Growing up as a dwarf person myself, by ten I had heard of the Seven Dwarfs, by thirteen the vile Mini-Me character had hit our screens, and three decades went by before I learned of Benjamin Lay.

One of the defining features of Rediker's book is how he addresses Lay's dwarfism. Other authors of historical biographies of defiant, gentle, and inspiring dwarf people have claimed to celebrate their subjects' lives while simultaneously insulting their bodies and diminishing their extraordinary struggles—without reviewers noticing or caring. Rediker does no such thing, seeking advice from the excellent Little People of America organization and explicitly acknowledging the "discrimination based on size and an often tyrannical normative image of the human body" our community experiences on a daily basis. As a proud and conscious dwarf person, as I finished reading that passage, I felt like a corset had been removed and oxygen filled my lungs.

Lay is not just a role model; he is a *dwarf* role model. When I have children—who are likely to have dwarfism, too—I will tell them bedtime stories of Lay's life and deeds. And on our bookshelves, a copy of Rediker's book, *The Fearless Benjamin Lay,* a celebratory and evidenced record of this great man, will await them.

LOVE MEANS NEVER HAVING TO SAY . . . ANYTHING

Jamison Hill

After dating Shannon for several months, I needed to say something to her, but I couldn't. It's not that I was nervous or unsure of the phrasing. It's that I couldn't speak. My lungs and larynx couldn't create the air pressure and vibrations needed to say the words floating around my mind.

This is our reality. I can't talk to Shannon about anything—not the weather or her day or how beautiful she is. Worst of all, I can't tell her I love her.

This was never a problem in my previous relationships with women I thought I loved or perhaps didn't love at all. These women knew my voice; they heard it every day. But they never knew what I was actually thinking.

They never knew how miserable my body felt because, back then, I was able to function at a relatively normal level and hide my illness well enough to seem healthy. I could go on dates, talk on the phone, and even drive to my girlfriend's house to spend the night.

But over time my condition worsened. Lyme disease had exacerbated my existing case of myalgic encephalomyelitis, an inflammatory multisystem disease that can leave patients unable to speak or eat for years at a time.

I'm now twenty-nine and have been sick for eight years, the last three of which I have spent bedridden, mostly speechless, and unable to eat solid food. I used to be a body builder who worked out for hours every day, and I was blindsided by the rapid deterioration of my health. I couldn't care for myself. I had to delay love and many other things while I waited for my health to stabilize.

That's when Shannon came into my life.

She lives in Ottawa, about two thousand miles from my house in California. We met online, which is common, but otherwise our relationship has no precedent or guide. We are two people very much in love but also very sick.

Shannon has the same condition I do. She has been sick longer, since adolescence, but thankfully has never lost her ability to speak. Instead, she struggles with unrelenting nausea and has trouble digesting food. She is often malnourished and her weight drops below a hundred pounds—too thin for someone five feet, five inches tall.

We both have low blood volume, which makes it difficult for her to walk without fainting and impossible for me to sit up in bed without intense pain and weakness.

Since I am bedridden, the only way we can be together is for her to travel across the continent to see me. But even with her willingness to jeopardize her health by traveling so far, we are often away from each other for months at a time.

When we are together, we spend weeks in bed, mostly holding each other, our bodies aligned like two pieces of a broken plate glued back together. Because I can't speak, we often resort to communicating by text messages while cuddling in bed.

It's like a monthlong sleepover and feels surreal, being stuck in a situation so miserable that it could make your skin crawl but finding comfort knowing that your soul mate is next to you, going through something similar.

But our experiences differ. Shannon can briefly get up to use the toilet, bathe, and, on a good day, make herself a meal. I, on the other hand, have to do everything in bed: brush my teeth, bathe, and use the "bathroom"—a plastic bag for bowel movements and, for urinating, a dubious-looking plastic container attached to a tube feeding into a bucket on the floor. These are not sexy things but are part of life—my life and ours together.

I was embarrassed at first to ask Shannon to avert her eyes and try not to think of me urinating inches from where we had been kissing just seconds earlier. But I have since come to realize that it's all part of sharing our lives. Knowing that nothing about my bedridden life makes Shannon uncomfortable endears her to me.

In contrast, I have had relationships with women who became upset at the first sign of anything inconvenient—one girlfriend who threatened to break up with me because she thought my beard trimmings were clogging the bathroom sink, and another who blamed our problems on my insomnia.

These failed romances remind me of the baffling incompatibilities two people can have, but also how love can transcend even the most insurmountable obstacles when you find the right person.

Before we started our relationship, when we were just two friends with the same illness texting for hours, I asked Shannon, "Do you think two sick people can be together?"

"Yes," she replied. "I think when you're both sick it makes it easier and harder at the same time."

"I guess the downside," I said, "is there's no healthy person to take care of you."

"But when you're alone, there's no healthy person to take care of you, either," she said.

I had never thought about it like that—the possibility of two sick people being in a successful relationship together. I have always assumed that one person in the couple would need to be healthy. Two sick people can't take care of each other.

But Shannon and I take care of each other in ways I never thought possible. I may not be able to make a meal for her, but I can have takeout delivered. And she may not be able to be my caregiver, but she can post an ad looking for one. We have done these things and many others for each other, from opposite ends of North America.

We share an empathy that only two people with the same condition can feel. We know what the other person is going through on bad days; we know how exasperating it is to explain invisible symptoms to doctors only to face skepticism. And we know all too well what it's like to be immobile in an ever-moving world.

Even so, we don't know everything about each other. We don't know what we were like as healthy people. We don't know what differences lie between our current selves and the people we were before getting sick—what maturation and emotional hardening have occurred during that transformation. Most fundamentally, we don't know what it's like to have a vocal conversation with each other.

Shannon has never heard my voice. She has never heard me berate a telemarketer or mumble to myself after making a typo. She has never heard me mess up a dinner toast or tell a corny joke. She has never heard me whisper into her ear or come up with a witty reply. She has never heard me ask a question or speak my mind, to anyone.

And she may never get to hear me do any of these things, but that's okay. Here is this lovely woman, devoid of judgment, who loves me for the words I type to her on my phone.

I never loved any of my previous girlfriends the way I love Shannon. I wanted to tell her how much her companionship means to me. I had tried before, many times, without success.

Still, I felt I had to try again. Somehow I had to convey, without typing, what I was feeling. My text messages were inadequate, and I thought about using hand signals, but the heart-shaped hand gesture felt far too clichéd.

So I tried to use my voice. To my surprise, for the first time in months, I heard actual sounds coming from my mouth. With my jaw locked, I whispered through clenched teeth, "I . . . love . . . you."

"What?" she said, startled.

I took a deep breath and fought back the nearly unbearable pain in my throat and jaw. Tears began to well up in my eyes. I whispered again, this time using all the strength I had: "I . . . love . . . you."

"Oh, sweetheart," she said. "I'm so sorry. I don't know what you're saying."

I wasn't sure what was worse: the emotional torment of not being able to speak or the physical pain of trying. After everything I had been through—the months of struggling to stay alive in my sickbed—and finally finding the love of my life, I couldn't tell Shannon that I loved her.

Lucky for me, I didn't have to. As if straight from a heart-wrenching scene in *Love Story,* Shannon took my hand, gave me a soft kiss, and said, "You don't have to say anything. I love you!"

Now, months later, it still holds true: for us, love means never having to say anything.

ON THE ANCESTRAL PLANE

Crip Hand-Me-Downs and the Legacy of Our Movements

Stacey Milbern

My favorite boots are socks. Crip socks. Because they are made out of brown leather to look like shoes, wearing them out in public as a wheelchair user is still socially acceptable. I loved these boot socks unabashedly and wore them every day until two years ago, when I slipped in the bathroom at work. I fell because socks, unlike actual shoes, do not have gripping soles (or soles in general). A nondisabled coworker had to check on me on the bathroom floor. No incident report filed, but it was disabled childhood humiliation relived all over again. I put the boots away, dismayed and furious at how much I let myself love shoes that could cause physical injury.

I don't have these kinds of strong feelings about all articles of clothing. These boot socks are special. These boots were worn by two of my personal heroes, crip elders who became crip ancestors when they passed: Harriet McBryde Johnson and Laura Hershey.

Harriet McBryde Johnson, an American writer and disability rights attorney, wore them in South Carolina. Her sister sewed these boots for her. Harriet's writing meant so much to me that Harriet is the secret name I've tucked away should I ever have the honor to name someone one day. When Harriet died, or maybe before, the shoes were gifted to her friend Laura Hershey in Colorado.

Laura, a disabled poet and brilliant feminist thinker, was/is equally remarkable. Her poetry describes experiences the majority of people can't fathom and still resonates with people from all kinds of backgrounds. She is one of my favorite poets, just as Harriet is one of my favorite authors. When Laura died, her partner, whom I did not know at the time, asked for my address. The boot socks arrived here in California two weeks later. I don't understand why I was the lucky recipient, but I am honored to be in this lineage. Wearing them made me feel powerful and good in my body. That's why I was so let down when I fell; it felt like my ancestors let me down.

Like my ancestors didn't know better, and it had an impact on me. It's not fair or reasonable to them, but it's how I felt.

I think about crip ancestorship often. It is tied to crip eldership for me, a related but different topic. So many disabled people live short lives, largely because of social determinants of health like lack of health care, inadequate housing, or unmet basic needs such as clean air and water. Other times the short lives are merely one truth of our bodyminds, like the neuromuscular conditions of Harriet, Laura, and myself. I do not know a lot about spirituality or what happens when we die, but my crip Korean life makes me believe that our earthly bodymind is but a fraction, and not considering our ancestors is electing to see only a glimpse of who we are. People sometimes assume ancestorship is reserved for those who are biologically related, but a cripped understanding of ancestorship holds that our deepest relationships are with people we choose to be connected to and honor day after day.

Ancestorship, like love, is expansive and breaks man-made boundaries cast upon it. My ancestors are disabled people who lived looking out of institution windows, wanting so much more for themselves. It's because of them that I know that when I reflect on the meaning of a "good life," an opportunity to contribute is as important as receiving the support one needs. My ancestors are people torn apart from loves by war and displacement. It's because of them I know the power of building home with whatever you have, wherever you are, whomever you are with. All of my ancestors know longing. Longing is often our connecting place.

I believe that our ancestors laugh, cry, hurt, rage, celebrate with us. Most important, I believe they learn as we are learning, just as we learn from them. We grow knowledge and movements with them. We crip futurism with them. We demand and entice the world to change the way things have always been done, with them. We change ourselves with them. They learn through us. When we become ancestors, we will also continue to learn.

I speculate that soon, our recently departed Carrie Ann Lucas, a lawyer, disability rights advocate, and activist who founded Disabled Parents Rights, an organization to fight discrimination against parents with disabilities, will settle into her ancestorship. She will remind people to be fierce and unapologetic in all things. She'll trail-blaze wherever she is, just as she did here. She will continue to transform how we think about the world and how to be in it, especially around the importance of showing up, loving hard, remembering ritual, giving

200 percent, believing in yourself and one another when others are foolish not to, creating the community/outfit/experience/vocation you wish for yourself. I wonder what she might learn from us, too.

I wear my boots. Not on days where I need to transfer standing on tile, but often. My ancestors and I are learning and loving. Together.

THE BEAUTY OF SPACES CREATED FOR AND BY DISABLED PEOPLE

s.e. smith

The theater is dim and just warm enough that I don't need my sweater, which I leave draped on the back of my creaky wooden seat. We are hushed, waiting for the lights to come up on the swooping ramp where the dance piece *Descent*, choreographed by Alice Sheppard in collaboration with Laurel Lawson, will be performed. This is one of my favorite parts of any theatrical production, the moment *before*, when anything might happen. Where all the barriers between us have fallen away.

Sheppard and then Lawson roll out, and they begin weaving intricate patterns with their bodies and wheelchairs while the music soars over them, with Michael

Maag's lighting and projection weaving around them. The audio describer speaks in a low, rhythmic voice that broadcasts to the whole room, interplaying with the performance and the music.

There is something weighty and sacred here.

It is very rare, as a disabled person, that I have an intense sense of belonging, of being not just tolerated or included in a space but actively owning it; "This space," I whisper to myself, "is for me." Next to me, I sense my friend has the same electrified feeling. This space is for us.

I am spellbound. I am also overwhelmed, feeling something swell in my throat as I look out across the crowd, to the wheelchair and scooter users at the front of the raked seating, the ASL interpreter in crisp black next to the stage. Canes dangle from seat backs, and a gilded prosthetic leg gleams under the safety lights. A blind woman in the row below me turns a tiny model of the stage over in her hands, tracing her fingers along with it in time to the audio description.

"I really wish I could have crammed all my disabled peeps in there," I say later.

Members of many marginalized groups have this shared experiential touchstone, this sense of unexpected and vivid belonging and an ardent desire to be able to pass this experience along. Some can remember the precise moment when they were in a space inhabited entirely by people like them for the first time. For disabled people, those spaces are often hospitals, group therapy sessions, and other clinical settings. That is often by design; we are kept isolated from one another, as though more than two disabled people in the same room will start a riot or make everyone feel awkward.

The first *social* setting where you come to the giddy understanding that this is a place for disabled people is a momentous one, and one worth lingering over. I cannot remember the first time it happened to me—perhaps a house party in San Francisco or an art show or a meeting of friends at a café. The experiences blend together, creating a sense of crip space, a communal belonging, a deep *rightness* that comes from not having to explain or justify your existence. They are resting points, even as they can be energizing and exhilarating.

Crip space is unique, a place where disability is celebrated and embraced—something radical and taboo in many parts of the world and sometimes even for people in those spaces. The idea that we need our own spaces, that we thrive in them, is particularly troubling for identities treated socially as a negative; why would you want to self-segregate with the other cripples? For those newly disabled, crip space may seem intimidating or frightening, with expectations that don't match the reality of experience—someone who has just experienced a tremendous life change is not always ready for disability pride or defiance, needing a kinder, gentler introduction.

The creation of spaces explicitly for marginalized people and not for others has been fraught with controversy. Proponents insist they're necessary for people to have intra-community conversations, and they create a safe environment for talking through complex issues. They also may say that people find them empowering, especially those who have been cut off from their community.

It isn't that nondisabled people are unwelcome at this dance performance. But the space has not been tailored to their needs and designed to seamlessly accommodate them, and they stand out. The experience pushes the boundaries of their understanding and expectations.

During the Q&A, the dancers roll forward and the ASL interpreter trails them.

"Any questions or comments?" one asks, the interpreter's hands moving swiftly in sync. The audience is momentarily frozen, as all audiences are at this question every time it is asked. The disabled people are still processing. We feel slightly giddy; this is a piece that speaks our common language, silently and beautifully, that reaches the deep parts of us we normally keep buttoned up and hidden away. The nondisabled people are hesitant, nervous, unsure about what to say in response to the work in progress we'd all been invited to witness.

"I liked . . . the ramp," one of the nondisabled people says hesitantly, gesturing at the set.

It must have been an unsettling experience, to be invited into our space. To be on the other side of the access divide. To see disabled people spreading their wings and soaring. To see wheelchairs turned into powerful extensions of dancers' bodies, enabling them to do things physically impossible for bipedal people.

Those in positions of power, evidently fearing that people are talking about them behind closed doors, persistently insist on barging into such spaces. They call these spaces divisive, and their organizers are told that they aren't valuing the contributions of allies. These bursts of petty outrage at stumbling upon one of the few places in the world that is not open to them inadvertently highlight exactly why such places are needed.

This is precisely *why* they are needed: as long as claiming our own ground is treated as an act of hostility, we need our ground. We need the sense of community for disabled people created in crip space. Yet, like any ground, it comes with soft spots and pitfalls, a reminder that the landscape is not uniform, can even become treacherous.

Even as some of us find a sense of belonging within

these corners of the world carved out for one another, not everyone feels welcome in them; disability is a broad sociocultural identity and experience, and not everyone thinks about disability in the same way. This can be the paradox of crip space: When do we exclude others in our zeal to embrace ourselves, with our refusal to consider the diversity of human experience? How can we cultivate spaces where everyone has that soaring sense of inclusion, where we can have difficult and meaningful conversations?

Crip space is akin to a fragile natural place. It must be protected in order to preserve the delicate things within, while remaining open to change with the seasons and the passage of time. That protection sometimes requires sacrifice or challenge, awkward questions, but that makes it no less vital. Because everyone deserves the shelter and embrace of crip space, to find their people and set down roots in a place they can call home.

After the dance, after the Q&A, after the drinks and snacks in the lobby, we must regretfully disperse back out into the chilly December night. The theater is in the Tenderloin, a San Francisco community in transition, and as we fan out across the sidewalk, we must return once more into the outside world, beyond crip space. The barriers begin to reappear.

A child across the street points at the phalanx of wheelchair users and says, "Look, Mommy!" Two adults stare, surprised when an adult wheelchair user unaccompanied by an attendant, braving the world alone, transfers into his car and slings his wheelchair into the backseat, pulling away from the curb with the quiet hum of an expensive German engine.

At the BART station around the corner, the elevators are, as usual, out of order.

© Eddie Hernandez Photography

ABOUT THE EDITOR

Alice Wong is a disabled activist, media maker, and research consultant based in San Francisco. She is the founder and director of the Disability Visibility Project, an online community created in 2014 dedicated to creating, sharing, and amplifying disability media and culture. Her memoir, *Year of the Tiger,* will be published by Vintage Books in 2022.

@SFdirewolf

ABOUT THE CONTRIBUTORS

Zipporah Arielle is a writer from a small town in Maine. She writes about everything, but her social justice work focuses primarily on issues revolving around disability, Queerness, and Jewishness. She currently resides in Nashville with her service dog in training, where she spends her days writing and ordering take-out. She plans to publish a book (or two) and spend as much of her life as possible traveling before retiring to the Italian countryside (or something like that).

Keah Brown is a journalist and writer whose work can be found in *Glamour, Marie Claire* UK, *Harper's Bazaar,* and *Teen Vogue,* among other publications. Her debut essay collection, *The Pretty One,* published in 2019, talks about her experiences as a young African American woman with cerebral palsy. You can learn more about her at keahbrown.com.

June Eric-Udorie is a twenty-year-old British writer and feminist activist. She is a cofounder of Youth for Change, an initiative that works to combat female genital mutilation and forced marriage around the world, and her advocacy has taken her to classrooms, the Southbank Centre's Women of the World Festival, and the United Nations. Her writing has appeared in *The Guardian, The Independent, ESPN the Magazine,* and *Fusion,* among other publications, and *Elle* UK named her Female Activist of the Year in 2017. She currently studies at Duke University, where she is a recipient of the University Scholars merit scholarship, established by Melinda French Gates.

The first Deafblind person to graduate from Harvard Law School, **Haben Girma** advocates for equal opportunities for people with disabilities. President Obama named her a White House Champion of Change. She received the Helen Keller Achievement Award and a spot on the Forbes "30 Under 30" list. President Bill Clinton, Prime Minister Justin Trudeau, and Chancellor Angela Merkel have all honored Haben. Haben believes disability is an opportunity for innovation. She travels the world teaching the benefits of choosing inclusion, and in 2019 she published her first book, *Haben: The Deafblind Woman Who Conquered Harvard Law.*

Eugene Grant is a writer and activist in the dwarfism and disability communities.

Ariel Henley is a writer in Northern California. She has written about issues related to beauty, equality, human connection, and trauma for outlets such as *The New York Times, The Washington Post,* and *The Atlantic.* She shares her story in an effort to eliminate the stigma surrounding disfigurement and to promote mainstream inclusion for individuals with physical differences. Her memoir, *A Face for Picasso,* is forthcoming from Farrar, Straus and Giroux.

A graduate of Sonoma State University, **Jamison Hill** has written essays for *The New York Times, The Washington Post, Men's Journal, the Los Angeles Times, Writer's Digest, Vox,* and *Vice.* Jamison was featured in *Forgotten Plague,* a documentary about myalgic encephalomyelitis, a devastating multisystem disease, as well as a Netflix original series about mysterious diseases. In 2019, Jamison's *New York Times* essay, "Love Means Never Having to Say . . . Anything," was adapted for WBUR Boston's *Modern Love* podcast and read by Pedro Pascal (*Game of Thrones* and *Narcos*). Jamison was also featured on Dax Shepard's *Armchair Expert* podcast.

Sandy Ho is a disability community organizer, activist, and disability policy researcher. She is the founder of the Disability & Intersectionality Summit, a biennial national conference organized by disabled activists that centers the experiences and knowledge of multiply marginalized disabled people. Sandy is a third of the team behind Access Is Love, a campaign copartnered with Alice Wong and Mia Mingus. Her areas of work include disability justice, racial justice, intersectionality, and disability studies. She is a disabled queer Asian American woman whose writing has been published by Bitch Media online.

Shoshana Kessock is CEO of Phoenix Outlaw Productions and a narrative lead at the immersive art installation Meow Wolf. She is a producer of live-action role-playing games, a contributor to dozens of tabletop role-playing games, the author of games like Dangers Untold and SERVICE, and a creator of multiple immersive events enjoyed worldwide. When she isn't producing live-action games, she writes fiction, comics, and screenplays. She hails from Brooklyn, New York, and is now living in Santa Fe, New Mexico, with her nineteen-year-old cat, Lilo. She can be found online at shoshanakessock.com or on Twitter at @ShoshanaKessock.

Lateef McLeod is a writer and a scholar. He earned a BA in English from the University of California, Berkeley, and an MFA in creative writing from Mills College. He published his first book of poetry, *A Declaration of a Body of Love,* in 2010, chronicling his life as a black man with a disability. He currently is writing a novel tentatively entitled *The Third Eye Is Crying* and is also completing another poetry book entitled *Whispers of Krip Love, Shouts of Krip Revolution.* More of his writing is available on his website, lateefhmcleod.com, and his HuffPost blog, huffpost.com/author/lateef-mcleod. You can also hear his perspective as a cohost of the podcast *Black Disabled Men Talk,* which can be heard on a variety of podcast platforms or via the website black disabledmentalk.com.

Stacey Milbern was an Oakland, California/Chochenyo Ohlone–based Disability Justice community organizer and writer. Her work was informed by her life experience as a mixed race (Korean and white) person, queer person, and disabled person with a nonnormative body. She believed our liberation requires us to be with one another and the earth interdependently. For her day job, she worked for a bank in corporate HR.

Mari Ramsawakh is a disabled and nonbinary writer, workshop facilitator, and podcaster. They have written for *Xtra*, Leafly, *Nuance*, and other publications. Their fiction has been published in the *Hart House Review* and *Toronto 2033*. Mari is also cohost and producer of the podcast *Sick Sad World*. They facilitate workshops related to disability, queerness, sexual health, and art, and they have spoken at 20:20: A Summit for the Students, by the Students; the Playground Conference; and the Make Change Conference. Mari's work is focused on increasing representation for racialized, queer, and disabled people in modeling, in all forms of media.

Alice Sheppard creates movement that challenges conventional understandings of disabled and dancing bodies. Engaging with disability arts, culture, and history, Alice attends to the complex intersections of disability, gender, and race. Alice is the founder and artistic lead for Kinetic Light, an ensemble working at the intersections of disability, dance, design, identity, and technology. Her writing has appeared in academic journals and *The New York Times*.

s.e. smith is a Northern California–based journalist and writer who has appeared in publications like *Esquire*, *Rolling Stone*, *In These Times*, *Bitch*, *The Nation*, *The Guardian*, and *Catapult*. Believing that liberation for some is justice for none, smith's work is rooted in provocative conversations and cultivating emerging writers.

Ricardo T. Thornton Sr. is a strong self-advocate in the District of Columbia and a former resident of the District's institution for people with disabilities, Forest Haven. He is copresident of Project ACTION!, an advocacy coalition of adults with disabilities, is an ambassador with the Special Olympics, and served on the President's Committee for People with Intellectual Disabilities. He has worked for more than forty years at the Martin Luther King Jr. Memorial Library. He is married to Donna, also a former resident of Forest Haven; they have one son and three grandchildren. The film *Profoundly Normal* chronicles their life as one of the first couples in the United States with developmental disabilities to marry.

Jeremy Woody was born in Omaha, Nebraska, and found out that he was profoundly Deaf when he was two years old, after which he learned to use American Sign Language. He attended the Iowa School for the Deaf until eighth grade, then moved to Georgia, where he was mainstreamed. He raced in National BMX races for more than seventeen years, from the time he was ten years old; he was the only Deaf competitor in the United States. He can be found on Twitter @2017JWoody and on Instagram @bmxcrazed67.

Maysoon Zayid is an actress, comedian, writer, and disability advocate. She is the cofounder/co–executive producer of the New York Arab-American Comedy Festival and has toured extensively at home and abroad. Maysoon is a commentator on CNN, authored "Find Another Dream" for Audible, and appears on *General Hospital*. Her talk, "I got 99 problems . . . palsy is just one," was the most viewed TED Talk of 2014.

In a time of destruction, create something.

—Maxine Hong Kingston

We urgently need to bring to our communities
the limitless capacity to love, serve, and create
for and with each other.

—Grace Lee Boggs

FURTHER READING

Nonfiction

Ballon, Emily Paige, Sharon daVanport, and Morénike Giwa Onaiwu, eds. *Sincerely, Your Autistic Child*. Boston: Beacon Press, 2021.

Brown, Keah. *The Pretty One: On Life, Pop Culture, Disability, and Other Reasons to Fall in Love with Me*. New York: Atria Books, 2019.

Piepzna-Samarasinha, Leah Lakshmi. *Care Work: Dreaming Disability Justice*. Vancouver, BC: Arsenal Pulp Press, 2018.

Fiction

Fritsch, Kelly, and Anne McGuire; Trejos, Eduardo (illus.). *We Move Together*. Illustrated by Eduardo Trejos. Chico, CA: AK Press, 2021.

Nijkamp, Marieke. *The Oracle Code: A Graphic Novel*. Illustrated by Manuel Preitano. Burbank, CA: DC Comics, 2020.

Anthologies

Cipriani, Belo Miguel, ed. *Firsts: Coming of Age Stores by People with Disabilities*. Minneapolis: OLEB Books, 2018.

Findlay, Carly, ed. *Growing Up Disabled in Australia*. Melbourne, Australia: Black Inc., 2021.

Jensen, Kelly, ed. *Body Talk: 37 Voices Explore Our Radical Anatomy*. Chapel Hill, NC: Algonquin Young Readers, 2020.

Jensen, Kelly, ed. *Don't Call Me Crazy: 33 Voices Start the Conversation About Mental Health*. Chapel Hill, NC: Algonquin Young Readers, 2018.

Luczak, Raymond, ed. *QDA: A Queer Disability Anthology*. Minneapolis: Squares and Rebels, 2015.

Nijkamp, Marieke, ed. *Unbroken: 13 Stories Starring Disabled Teens*. New York: Farrar, Straus, and Giroux, 2018.

Wong, Alice, ed. *Resistance and Hope: Essays by Disabled People*. Pacific Grove, CA: Smashwords, 2018.

PERMISSION ACKNOWLEDGMENTS

"Selma Blair Became a Disabled Icon Overnight. Here's Why We Need More Stories Like Hers" by Zipporah Arielle first appeared on *Bustle* on March 6, 2019. Copyrighted 2019. Bustle Digital Group. 2134966:1219AT.

"When You Are Waiting to Be Healed" by June Eric-Udorie first appeared on *Catapult* on September 22, 2016. Reprinted with permission of the author.

"Guide dogs don't lead blind people. We wander as one." by Haben Girma first appeared in *The Washington Post* on August 7, 2019. Including excerpts from *Haben: The Deafblind Woman Who Conquered Harvard Law* by Haben Girma, copyright © 2019 by Haben Girma, originally published by Twelve Books, an imprint of Hachette Book Group, Inc., New York, in 2019. Reprinted by permission of Haben Girma and Twelve Books, an imprint of Hachette Book Group, Inc.

"The Fearless Benjamin Lay—Activist, Abolitionist, Dwarf Person" by Eugene Grant first appeared on *The Beacon Broadside* on April 26, 2018. Reprinted with permission of the author.

"There's a Mathematical Equation That Proves I'm Ugly—Or So I Learned in My Seventh Grade Art Class" by Ariel Henley first appeared on *Narratively* on July 18, 2016. Reprinted with permission of the author.

"Love Means Never Having to Say . . . Anything" by Jamison Hill first appeared in *The New York Times* on May 25, 2018. From *The New York Times*. © 2018 The New York Times Company. All rights reserved. Used under license.

"Canfei to Canji: The Freedom to be Loud" by Sandy Ho first appeared on bitchmedia.org on August 1, 2018. Reprinted with permission of Bitch Media.

"Falling/Burning: Hannah Gadsby, *Nanette,* and Being a Bipolar Creator" by Shoshana Kessock first appeared on ShoshanaKessock.com on July 12, 2018. Reprinted with permission of the author.

"Gaining Power through Communication Access" by Lateef McLeod first appeared on "Assistive Technology," *Disability Visibility* podcast, Episode 3, on October 1, 2017. Reprinted with permission of the author.

"On the Ancestral Plane: Crip Hand-Me-Downs and the Legacy of Our Movements" by Stacey Park Milbern first appeared on the Disability Visibility Project, March 10, 2019. Reprinted with permission of the author.

"Incontinence Is a Public Health Issue—and We Need to Talk About It" by Mari Ramsawakh first appeared on *Them* on January 4, 2019. Reprinted with permission of the author.

"The Beauty of Spaces Created for and by Disabled People" by s.e. smith first appeared on *Catapult* on October 22, 2018. Reprinted with permission of author.

"We Can't Go Back" by Ricardo T. Thornton Sr. first appeared as "Statement of Ricardo Thornton Sr. Before the U.S. Senate, Committee on Health, Education, Labor and Pensions Regarding Olmstead Enforcement Update: Using the ADA to Promote Community Integration," on June 21, 2012. Reprinted by permission of the author.

"The Isolation of Being Deaf in Prison" by Jeremy Woody, as told to Christie Thompson, first appeared on the Marshall Project on October 18, 2018. Reprinted by permission of the author.

"If You Can't Fast, Give" by Maysoon Zayid first appeared on Maysoon.com on June 20, 2015. Reprinted by permission of the author.